Napa Valley
ICONIC WINERIES

NOTEWORTHY WINES & ARTISAN VINTNERS
Photography by M. J. Wickham

Published by

PANACHE
PANACHE PARTNERS

Published by

Panache Partners, LLC
1424 Gables Court
Plano, TX 75075
469.246.6060
Fax: 469.246.6062
www.panache.com

Publishers: Brian G. Carabet and John A. Shand

Copyright © 2012 by Panache Partners, LLC
All rights reserved.

No part of this book may be reproduced or transmitted in any form or by any means, electronic or mechanical, including photocopying, recording, or by any information storage or retrieval system, except brief excerpts for the purpose of review, without written permission of the publisher.

All images in this book have been reproduced with the knowledge and prior consent of the professionals concerned and no responsibility is accepted by the producer, publisher, or printer for any infringement of copyright or otherwise arising from the contents of this publication. Every effort has been made to ensure that credits accurately comply with the information supplied.

Printed in Canada

Distributed by Independent Publishers Group
800.888.4741

PUBLISHER'S DATA

Napa Valley Iconic Winereis

Library of Congress Control Number: 2012930879

ISBN 13: 978-0-9832398-3-3
ISBN 10: 983239835

First Printing 2012

10 9 8 7 6 5 4 3 2 1

Right: Round Pond Estate, page 165

Previous Page: Keenan Winery, page 117

This publication is intended to showcase the work of extremely talented people. The publisher does not require, warrant, endorse, or verify any professional accreditations, educational backgrounds, or professional affiliations of the individuals or firms included herein. All copy and photography published herein has been reviewed and approved as free of any usage fees or rights and accurate by the individuals and/or firms included herein.

Panache Partners, LLC. is dedicated to the restoration and conservation of the environment. Our books are manufactured with strict adherence to an environmental management system in accordance with ISO 14001 standards, including the use of paper from mills certified to derive their products from well-managed forests. We are committed to continued investigation of alternative paper products and environmentally responsible manufacturing processes to ensure the preservation of our fragile planet.

Napa Valley
ICONIC WINERIES

Silver Oak Cellars, page 181

FOREWORD

Napa Valley's food and wine possess a sense of place and a sense of taste. This is California—the West. Although it's no longer wild, the state remains a land of experimentation and exploration. Napa Valley is no different; it's a land of bold flavors where cuisine and wines come from the soil up to the chef and the vintner. It is a unique character that's not about the artist, but about the art itself.

As you tour Napa Valley, you acquire this sense of taste, this sense of terroir: the combination of soil and climate that impacts the flavor of the grapes. Strangers almost instantly become friends as they meet in the tasting rooms of established and new wineries alike. They trade stories and develop a bond over the bright red pinot noirs, the deep black cabernet sauvignons, and the crisp, clear chardonnays that come out of the valley. And when they return home, the memories and flavor of Napa follow them there.

There's a difference between taste and flavor. Wines from regions around the globe have brilliant tastes, but Napa wines possess a flavor, a spirit, that you can't find anywhere else. It creates a lore about the region—people who have never set foot on the sloped hills and luscious valleys idolize it. And once you visit, you realize the qualities of life and light associated with Napa are everyday occurrences. You taste this in the wines of Napa Valley, and you taste the vintner's personality in the glass.

Winemaking in Napa Valley is relatively young, but it stands as a testament to the dedication, adventurism, and true talent of vintners in this small, verdant stretch of land. Here, food and wine go hand in hand, and are always more enjoyable with family and friends.

This is what Napa Valley wines are all about—vitality, experimentation, and a true joie de vivre. Sit back with your favorite glass and enjoy this wonderful collection of wineries that make Napa Valley great.

Cheers and bon appétit,

Michael Chiarello
Chef, vintner, and TV host

Photograph courtesy of Michael Chiarello

INTRODUCTION

Think about Napa Valley, and images of rolling hills with flourishing, sun-kissed grapes blanketed by a morning fog come to mind. With the area's stellar international reputation in mind, it's easy to imagine that friends have been gathering around their favorite bottles of cabernet for generations, but the idyllic lifestyle of Napa Valley winemaking is relatively young. What began as a small fraternity of winemakers in the 1880s was reborn following Prohibition in the 1930s, before experiencing a world-changing renaissance in the 1970s that truly put the region on the global wine map.

The magic of Napa Valley is contagious; you can't help but fall in love with its fertile lands and welcoming people. This book will take you on an exclusive journey of this breathtaking region, sharing the insights and creations of the gifted vintners and proprietors who helped usher this now-famous area onto the world stage. Experience the magnificent panoramas of the valley floor and mountainside vineyards where some of America's—and even the world's—best grapes are grown. Share in the stories of winemakers, from those who inherited their family's legacy to vintners who took a decidedly non-traditional approach. Learn about the finest producers and labels the valley has to offer and discover the best ways to enjoy these delectable wines.

In *Napa Valley Iconic Wineries,* we chart the evolution of the region's wine industry, featuring the trailblazers and newcomers who have helped make the area's wines the culinary and cultural phenomenon they are today. It is a special book, filled with insights of winemakers, tasting notes for their signature bottlings and flagship wines, enticing food and wine pairings, additional interactive features through QR code technology, and glimpses into the personal lives of Napa Valley's iconic leaders. Enjoy your invitation to Napa Valley, where there's a bottle with your name on it.

Cheers!

Carla and Peter Bowers
Associate Publishers

Photograph by M. J. Wickham

Taylor Lombardo Architects, page 235

HISTORY

Napa Valley's storied past tells a tale of both hardship and victory as the area endeavored to establish itself as a successful wine-producing region. With a dedication to the art and craft of winemaking, the area became globally recognized for its unparalleled varietals. Carrying forth the tradition of excellence, Napa continues to produce award-winning wines that guarantee a long and prosperous future. With the help of The Napa Valley Appellation Education Program and Napa Valley Vintners, dig further into the region's unique history with videos accessible by scanning the QR codes with your smartphone or mobile device.

NAPA VALLEY ROCKS: Napa Valley
Explore the topography of Napa Valley.

1769
SPANISH BEGIN TO SETTLE IN CALIFORNIA: Father Junipero Serra plants mission vines at Mission San Diego. In 1772, he makes California's first vintage.

1810-1821
MEXICAN WAR OF INDEPENDENCE: Under Mexican rule, ranching and trade increase while the missions—and winemaking—decrease in importance.

NAPA VALLEY ROCKS: History
Learn more about the early history of Napa Valley.

1872
PHYLLOXERA IS DISCOVERED IN NAPA VALLEY: Phylloxera, a vine-destroying insect, hits the blossoming vine industry. Every remedy is tried—including the use of flooding and poisonous gasses—to rid the valley of the pest. Fewer than half of the vines planted in the 1800s survive into the next century.

1920
PROHIBITION BECOMES LAW: Mandated by the 18th Amendment, Prohibition bans the sale, manufacture, and transportation of alcohol.

1944
NAPA VALLEY VINTNERS IS FORMED: A group of vintners come together to share ideas on grape growing and winemaking, and evolve into Napa Valley Vintners, the trade organization dedicated to advancing Napa Valley wines.

1966
ROBERT MONDAVI OPENS WINERY: Breaking away from his family's Charles Krug estate, Mondavi founds the first new, large-scale winery established in the valley since Prohibition. The number of wineries in the region begins to rapidly grow.

NAPA VALLEY ROCKS: Vintner Leadership
Discover the environmental initiatives enacted by Napa Valley Vintners.

1981
FIRST NAPA VALLEY AUCTION HELD: The annual celebration of Napa Valley wine develops over the years to be the world's most successful wine charity event.

1530-1603
EARLY EUROPEAN EXPLORATION: The first European explorers sail along the coast of California on their way to Asia.

1603
LA PUNTA DE LOS REYES APPEARS ON SPANISH MAPS: Modern day Point Reyes, California, appears on Spanish maps as a point of reference for sailors.

NAPA VALLEY ROCKS: Climate
Find out why the climate in Napa Valley is idyllic for grape growing.

1838
GEORGE C. YOUNT PLANTS FIRST VINES IN NAPA VALLEY: For his carpentry work under General Mariano Vallejo, Yount receives the Rancho Caymus land grant in 1836, becomes the first settler in Napa Valley, and plants the first vitis vinifera vines.

1861
CHARLES KRUG ESTABLISHES THE FIRST WINERY IN NAPA VALLEY: Charles Krug receives 540 acres of land north of St. Helena as dowry from his wife, Carolina Bale. Krug founds his winery in 1861 and introduces the use of a cider press and the careful selection of growing sites.

1889
OVER 140 WINERIES OPERATE IN NAPA VALLEY: By 1889, more than 140 wineries are in operation in Napa Valley. Prices plummet in the flooded market. The concentrated surplus of grapes, combined with the phylloxera outbreak, cause many of the valley's wineries to close.

1933
PROHIBITION IS REPEALED: With the 21st Amendment, Prohibition is repealed.

NAPA VALLEY ROCKS: Geology and Soils
Get a glimpse of the varied soils in Napa Valley.

1968
NAPA VALLEY AGRICULTURAL PRESERVE ESTABLISHED: Prompted by local vintners and civil leaders, the California legislature gives tax relief to landowners designating their land for agricultural purposes. Stretching between Napa and Calistoga, it is the first preserve of its kind in the state.

1976
JUDGMENT OF PARIS: A competition organized by British wine merchant Steven Spurrier, the Paris Wine Tasting of 1976—also called the Judgment of Paris—pits California wines against French vintages. To the surprised French winemakers, a California wine rates best in each category.

NAPA VALLEY

Beaulieu Vineyard	13	Gargiulo Vineyards	83
Blankiet Estate	17	Grgich Hills Estate	89
Cakebread Cellars	25	Heitz Wine Cellars	95
Castello di Amorosa	33	Hill Family Estate	103
Caymus Vineyards	43	Inglenook	109
Chappellet Vineyard & Winery	51	Joseph Phelps Vineyards	113
David Arthur Vineyards	57	Keenan Winery	117
Del Dotto Winery	61	Kenzo Estate	123
Domaine Carneros	69	Morlet Family Vineyards & Winery	129
Fantesca Estate & Winery	73	Mumm Napa	135
Frog's Leap	79	O'Connell Family Vineyard	141

Shafer Vineyards, page 169

Peju Province Winery	.147	Trefethen Family Vineyards	.205
Robert Mondavi Winery	.153	Twomey Cellars	.211
Rombauer Vineyards	.159	Vineyard 7&8	.215
Round Pond Estate	.165	Vineyard 29	.219
Shafer Vineyards	.169	ZD Wines	.225
Sherwin Family Vineyards	.173		
Signorello Estate	.177		
Silver Oak Cellars	.181		
Silverado Vineyards	.187		
Spring Mountain Vineyard	.193		
Staglin Family Vineyard	.199		

OFF THE VINE

Seguin Moreau Napa Cooperage 231

Taylor Lombardo Architects 235

Beaulieu Vineyard RUTHERFORD

When Georges de Latour and his wife Fernande first laid eyes on the land that would become Beaulieu Vineyard, she exclaimed, "*Quel beau lieu!*" Translated to "what a beautiful place," the expression became the name of the vineyard when Georges founded it in 1900. With a vision of making Napa Valley wines to rival those of his native France, Georges quickly made a name for himself by importing phylloxera-resistant rootstock from Europe. Soon thereafter, Beaulieu Vineyard began selling wine to the Catholic Church—a strong relationship that allowed the winery to be one of the few in Napa Valley to remain in business through Prohibition. In 1938, enologist André Tchelistcheff joined Beaulieu Vineyard, introducing cold fermentation for white wines, malolactic fermentation and French oak aging for reds.

ABOVE: The winery's historic redwood doors; the building was originally constructed in 1885.

FACING PAGE: Beaulieu Vineyard Ranch No. 1 is the original Beaulieu Vineyard property, in the heart of the Rutherford Bench. It was purchased by Georges de Latour in 1904.
Photographs by M. J. Wickham

GEORGES DE LATOUR
PRIVATE RESERVE CABERNET SAUVIGNON

GOURMET PAIRINGS
Rich meats such as filet mignon and venison pair perfectly with the richness and complexity of the wine, playing exquisitely against the wine's supple cocoa finish.

TASTING NOTES
Exceptionally complex, the wine boasts deep aromas and expansive flavors of black licorice, cassis, blackberry, dark plum, mocha, and toasted oak spices. With an opulent dark-fruit and new-oak character, it is supple with robust tannins. It has stood as the benchmark cabernet sauvignon from Rutherford since its inaugural vintage in 1936.

WINEMAKER'S INSIGHT
We hand-select fruit from our finest cabernet sauvignon vines in our BV Ranches No. 1 and No. 2, which were originally planted by Georges de Latour in the early 1900s. More than a century of growing grapes has given us the knowledge to match the best rootstocks, clones, and cultivation techniques to create this exceptional wine. In our state-of-the-art winery, dedicated to the production of this wine, 40 percent of the must, or crushed grapes, barrel ferments in new French oak barrels, with the balance in open-top fermenters.

TECHNICAL DATA

APPELLATION: Rutherford
COMPOSITION: A predominantly cabernet sauvignon-led blend, typically blended with other classic Bordeaux varietals
MATURATION: Over 20 months in new French oak barrels
CELLARING: Exceptional now, but will age beautifully for several decades
WEBSITE: www.bvwines.com

LEARN MORE

Learn more about Beaulieu Vineyard.

Beaulieu Vineyard's primary focus is cabernet sauvignon, and the Georges de Latour Private Reserve Cabernet Sauvignon—the legacy of the family's private collection—became Napa Valley's first cabernet with a cult following. Other varietals produced with a dedication to time-honored tradition combined with use of the latest winemaking technology include merlot, pinot noir, chardonnay, and red blends. Under the direction of winemaker Jeffrey Stambor, the lush flavors of Napa Valley grapes transform into distinctive wines as a true tribute to the region.

TOP: Director of winemaking Jeffrey Stambor stands in Beaulieu Vineyard's new state-of-the-art reserve winery, dedicated to the production of Georges de Latour Private Reserve Cabernet Sauvignon.

ABOVE: The reserve tasting room features Beaulieu Vineyard's reserve wines, including a Georges de Latour library collection with wines dating back to 1970.

LEFT: Historical tours include a visit to the Heritage Room, a collection that features historical winemaking equipment and memorabilia documenting the early days of the winery.
Photographs by M. J. Wickham

FACING PAGE LEFT: *Photograph by M. J. Wickham*
FACING PAGE RIGHT: *Photograph © iStockphoto.com/visual7*

Blankiet Estate YOUNTVILLE

Ideally situated in the Mayacamas Mountain Range, Blankiet Estate's Paradise Hills Vineyards spread across three knolls on the western hills above Yountville. The magnificent land overlooks the historic Napanook vineyard, planted in 1836 and the oldest parcel in Napa. After years of searching, Claude and Katherine Blankiet established Blankiet Estate in 1996, hiring viticulturist David Abreu to plant the 16-acre vineyard; the venture impressed the legendary Helen Turley so much that she signed on as winemaker. Blankiet continues to produce extraordinary, highly coveted

ABOVE: The classic gated entrance to Blankiet Estate.

FACING PAGE: Sunrise over the winery at Blankiet Estate in Yountville.
Photographs by Kurt-Inge Eklund

wines, just as it has since its inaugural 1999 vintage. From Helen Turley, Martha McClellan, and David Abreu to Michel Rolland, the winemakers, viticulture experts, and enologists consulting and contributing to Blankiet have all been superstars. Current winemaker Denis Malbec—former cellar master at Château Latour—crafts fewer than a thousand cases per year of two flagship proprietary red wines, one a predominantly

ABOVE: The Renaissance-style vaulted ceiling in the foyer of the Castello di Paradiso, painted by Mark Marthaler, is a faithful reproduction of Old World craftsmanship.
Photograph by Claude Blankiet

TOP RIGHT: Castello di Paradiso and its magnificently landscaped grounds.
Photograph by Claude Blankiet

RIGHT: Wine ages for two years in 100-percent French oak barrels in the Blankiet Estates caves.
Photograph by Claude Blankiet

FACING PAGE: The Castello di Paradiso's 65-foot-high tower envelops an interior staircase escalier de vis, with 88 steps and seven spirals leading to the top.
Photograph by Peter Bowers

cabernet sauvignon blend and the other a St.-Emilion-inspired assemblage of merlot and cabernet franc.

Under the companion label Prince of Hearts is a rosé, barrel fermented and aged in French oak for a year, as well as a cabernet sauvignon assembled from barrels not selected for the flagship cuvées. In the state-of-the-art winery, 100-percent new French oak barrels age the wines exclusively, and nothing is ever fined or filtered. The final blend will always be the one that most vividly expresses the character of the land and the nuances of each vintage.

Within four separate micro-climates with their own soil conditions, eight blocks and 30 micro-blocks compose the vineyard. Tightly planting the vines—about 2,400 vines per acre—entices competition and a deeper root system. Sustainable farming and micro-harvesting ensure that optimum phenolic maturity is attained. Both Claude and Katherine supervise the three sorting tables, patiently processing only three-fourths of a ton per hour to ensure that only pristine berries go in the fermentation tanks.

A Burgundy native, Claude applies a distinctive pioneering spirit to his winery; Blankiet innovations include a misting system to control summer heat spikes and special shading material to protect the fruit from excess solar radiation. Claude's relentless drive to excel underwrites much of Blankiet Estate's success.

LEFT: Early morning fog rises above the Paradise Hills Vineyard and olive trees at Blankiet Estate.
Photograph by Peter Bowers

THIS PAGE: Photograph by M. J. Wickham
FACING PAGE LEFT: Photograph © iStockphoto.com/robynmac
FACING PAGE RIGHT: Photograph © iStockphoto.com/maribee

BLANKIET ESTATE RIVE DROITE RED

GOURMET PAIRINGS
Pair with a rack of spring lamb garnished with new potatoes roasted in duck fat, garlic, and rosemary.

TASTING NOTES
As Stephen Tanzer notes in his *International Wine Cellar* review, the "beautiful California merlot" boasts a "perfumed nose of currant, cherry, cocoa powder, brown spices, and rose petal." Extremely approachable, the layers of freshness make it light and rich, but the strong flavors lend it a further depth. Soft, round, and structured, the vintage will age extremely well.

WINEMAKER'S INSIGHT
The wine's name is in homage to the right bank of Bordeaux, St.-Emilion and Pomerol, where merlot is the king of grapes. We believe that our Paradise Hills clay site is one of the best merlot sources in the United States.

TECHNICAL DATA
APPELLATION: Yountville
COMPOSITION: 80% merlot, 12% cabernet franc, 8% cabernet sauvignon
MATURATION: Aged for two years in 100% French oak barrels
CELLARING: Delicious now but can be cellared for up to 30 years
WEBSITE: www.blankiet.com

BLANKIET ESTATE PROPRIETARY RED

GOURMET PAIRINGS
The wine tastes wonderful with beef short ribs marinated for two days in red wine—the better the wine, the better the sauce—and then slowly braised.

TASTING NOTES
Called "a brilliant, full-throttle, complex effort... similar to a top-flight Graves from Bordeaux" by Robert Parker, the wine has notes of crème de cassis and blackberry. Full-bodied and full of dark fruit, the wine's pronounced minerality gives a firm structure to the complex and concentrated product.

WINEMAKER'S INSIGHT
Harvest spans over 45 days and usually occurs over 14 separate grape pickings, done at night to preserve the freshness of flavors, and sorted carefully on 50-foot sorting tables manned by 28 people. Grapes are vinified in small stainless steel tanks and in French oak barrels. Uncrushed berries are cold-macerated for a week, then fermented with precise temperature control followed by an extended skin maceration. The merlot is also barrel-fermented.

TECHNICAL DATA
APPELLATION: Yountville
COMPOSITION: Cabernet sauvignon with merlot, cabernet franc, petit verdot
MATURATION: Aged for two years in 100% French oak barrels
CELLARING: Delicious now but can be cellared for up to 30 years
WEBSITE: www.blankiet.com

LEARN MORE

Learn more about Blankiet Estate.

Cakebread Cellars RUTHERFORD

One of the biggest names in Napa, the Cakebread family's foray into winemaking originally began with photography. In the early 1970s, Jack Cakebread—who had studied with Ansel Adams—came to Napa as a book photographer. He visited family friends with Rutherford ranch property, inquired about buying it, and by the end of the day a deal had been negotiated. Cakebread Cellars took shape as Jack, wife Dolores, and their family began driving up to work on the ranch every weekend after putting in a week's worth of work at the family auto shop. The first vintage, 1973 chardonnay in 157 cases, sold to the burgeoning Bay Area premium wine enthusiasts attracting attention to the region, and nowadays Cakebread

ABOVE: The exterior of Cakebread Cellars in Rutherford, California.
FACING PAGE: Foster Road Vineyards.
Photographs by Terrence McCarthy

DANCING BEAR RANCH ON HOWELL MOUNTAIN CABERNET SAUVIGNON

GOURMET PAIRINGS

To match the intensity of the wine's lush dark fruit and firm integrated tannins, pair it with herbed, grilled rack of lamb. The seasoning suits the wine's spice, rich cocoa, and warm vanilla notes.

TASTING NOTES

The mountain wine's trademark is an intriguing dance of intensity and elegance. High-toned aromas of freshly crushed boysenberries, dark cherries, and forest-floor spice introduce a dense, tightly wound palate packed with marvelously rich and concentrated black cherry, boysenberry, and blackberry flavors, which are enhanced by savory clove, cocoa, and vanilla tones.

WINEMAKER'S INSIGHT

The winemaker's challenge is to capture the intense mountain character of the fruit without extracting overly aggressive tannins. The approach entails constantly monitoring tannin levels in the wine during fermentation and maceration. Co-fermenting a portion of the cabernet sauvignon and cabernet franc also helps to soften the former's tannins and enhance the wine's complexity.

TECHNICAL DATA

APPELLATION: Howell Mountain
COMPOSITION: Cabernet sauvignon, cabernet franc
MATURATION: 21 months in French oak
CELLARING: Will delight wine lovers now and over the next decade
WEBSITE: www.cakebread.com

LEARN MORE

Learn more about Cakebread Cellars.

Cellars is one of the foremost stops in Wine Country. Cakebread also played a pivotal role in increasing the focus of wine and food pairings, and in encouraging the movement toward making those edible accompaniments out of local ingredients. What seems natural and expected today was a very new concept in the 1980s, and Cakebread had the foresight to position itself at the forefront of those changes. Dolores oversees hospitality and her organic kitchen garden, and organized with Jack and hotelier Bill Shoaf the first four-day American Harvest Workshop seminar in 1986, which placed a greater focus on wine as part of the meal while inviting top chefs to interact with winemakers and local farmers. The Cakebreads have always believed wine has a place in a healthy, balanced diet, and their belief has now spread as a result of

ABOVE LEFT & BOTTOM: Cakebread Cellars Dancing Bear Ranch on Howell Mountain.
Photographs by Andy Katz

TOP: Dennis, Jack, Dolores, and Bruce Cakebread.
Photograph by Terrence McCarthy

FACING PAGE LEFT: *Photograph by M. J. Wickham*
FACING PAGE RIGHT: *Photograph by Terrence McCarthy*

their efforts.

Jack's sons run the winery today. Former winemaker Bruce Cakebread became president and COO, while vice-chairman Dennis heads up sales and marketing.

How to best harvest the grapes has also been fine-tuned into a science. A neutron-probe irrigation system allots water to only the vines that need it to grow the best grapes. During the summer the vineyard team comes up with a game plan for each block, detailing how to press, fermentation instructions, and which barrels to use based on previous data and season projections, all

ABOVE: Cakebread Cellars Foster Road Vineyards.
Photograph by Terrence McCarthy

LEFT: Cakebread Cellars Milton Road Vineyard.
Photograph by Steven Rothfeld

FACING PAGE LEFT: *Photograph by Terrence McCarthy*
FACING PAGE RIGHT: *Photograph by M. J. Wickham*

NAPA VALLEY CABERNET SAUVIGNON

GOURMET PAIRINGS

The wine goes best with smoked tri-tip rubbed in ancho chile and coffee to match the intense blackberry, plum, and black cherry flavors of the wine, topped with a sun-dried cherry and pomegranate sauce.

TASTING NOTES

The pretty nose is redolent with boysenberry and blackberry scents joined by hints of wild cherry, loamy earth, and oak vanillin. On the supple, beautifully structured palate, the wine offers rich black cherry flavors framed by perfectly integrated tannins and a long, savory finish.

WINEMAKER'S INSIGHT

We lavish specialized care on each component of the blend to increase the quality. Each vintage consists of several distinct lots of grapes, processed separately. Each lot is cold-soaked prior to fermentation for 36 to 48 hours. We then ferment and age the lots separately, tailoring tank size, yeast strain, fermentation temperature, and barrel type to the fruit character of each lot. Aging in oak barrels, some vintages go to 20 months.

TECHNICAL DATA

APPELLATION: Napa Valley
COMPOSITION: Cabernet sauvignon, merlot, cabernet franc, petit verdot, malbec
MATURATION: 20 months in French oak barrels
CELLARING: Delicious now; will develop further nuances with another five to seven years' bottle age
WEBSITE: www.cakebread.com

WATCH A VIDEO

President Bruce Cakebread talks about the roundness and aging potential of Cakebread Cellars' Napa Valley Cabernet Sauvignon.

NAPA VALLEY CHARDONNAY

GOURMET PAIRINGS
Posole verde—with the broth's fresh, bright flavors from the tomatillos and cilantro, as well as the sweetness of the corn—enhances the ripe apple, melon, and citrus flavors of the wine.

TASTING NOTES
The wine boasts an attractive, light golden-straw color and fresh, lightly buttery, ripe golden apple, pear, and citrus aromas, complemented by seductive vanilla and cinnamon–nutmeg scents from oak aging and subtle yeast tones from lees contact. Lush, concentrated, and creamy on the palate, the melon and baking spice flavors culminate in a long, beautifully structured finish boasting crisp acidity and zesty mineral tones.

WINEMAKER'S INSIGHT
Our chardonnay winemaking regimen is predicated on night harvesting, which ensures the grapes are picked cold and retain their fruit purity and bright natural acidity. The fruit is whole-cluster-pressed, further preserving freshness and purity. All but a small percentage of the component wines age in barrel for eight months on the yeast lees, with periodic stirring, to enhance texture and richness while preserving full varietal expression.

TECHNICAL DATA

APPELLATION: Napa Valley
COMPOSITION: 100% chardonnay
MATURATION: Eight months in French oak barrels, with periodic stirring of the lees
CELLARING: Delicious now, but will handsomely reward another three to five years' bottle aging
WEBSITE: www.cakebread.com

LEARN MORE

Learn more about Cakebread Cellars.

to maximize the fruit.

The portfolio explores now-famous Napa specialties like single-vineyard cabernet sauvignons, pinot noirs, and chardonnays, as well as top-flight sauvignon blanc, merlot, syrah, and zinfandel offerings, along with red blend Rubáiyat, dry rosé Vin de Porche, and Dancing Bear Ranch on Howell Mountain. All have garnered numerous accolades and remain highly sought after by the most discerning collectors. Cakebread Cellars, fortunately established during the early years, has earned a place among the Napa greats.

ABOVE: Sweeping vineyard views can be seen from the balcony tasting room.

RIGHT: The barrel room stores Cakebread Cellars' renowned wines.
Photographs by M. J. Wickham

FACING PAGE LEFT: *Photograph by M. J. Wickham*
FACING PAGE RIGHT: *Photograph by Terrence McCarthy*

Castello di Amorosa   CALISTOGA

Overlooking the Napa Valley in Calistoga is an authentically styled Tuscan castle and winery. Painstakingly built over 15 years by vintner Dario Sattui to be true to Old World style, the 13th-century castle offers visitors the chance to taste wines in the same castle where they were made, in accordance with European tradition. A lifelong aficionado of medieval architecture and great-grandson of the man who founded one of San Francisco's oldest wineries, Dario sees his passions united in Castello di Amorosa. After reviving the family winery, he spent years researching and touring castles in Italy while dreaming and sketching plans for a castle of his own. The dream ballooned over the years into the 121,000-square-foot structure that stands so majestically today, complete with five defensive

ABOVE: The Castello is stunning even from the air.
Photograph courtesy of Castello di Amorosa

FACING PAGE: The morning sun greets the Castello and moat—an architectural masterpiece.
Photograph by Jim Sullivan

TOP: The courtyard at dusk.
Photograph by Peter Menzel

ABOVE: The North Tower stands tall above the Castello's Diamond Mountain District vineyards.
Photograph by Jim Sullivan

RIGHT: A refreshing storm passes and afternoon sun highlights the courtyard's Tuscan arches.
Photograph by Jim Sullivan

FACING PAGE LEFT: *Photograph © iStockphoto.com/vfoto*
FACING PAGE RIGHT: *Photograph by Jim Sullivan*

IL BARONE RESERVE CABERNET SAUVIGNON NAPA VALLEY

GOURMET PAIRINGS
The grand, bold flavors pair well with grilled or delectably sauced red and game meats, and vegetables. Wonderful with dark chocolate.

TASTING NOTES
Dense and darkly pigmented, the wine possesses subtle aromas of sweet oak, savory spices, and black fruit: blackberries, juicy currants, and black cherry. Its supple tannins and full flavors, with an enduring fruit focus on the finish, create a palate rich and well structured. The acidity is enough to keep the finish fresh and clean—the perfect accompaniment to rich foods.

WINEMAKER'S INSIGHT
Positioned to take full advantage of warm, morning sun, Castello di Amorosa's up-valley, high-elevation hillside vineyards are located in the heart of the Napa Valley's Diamond Mountain District, a grape growing area known for its rich, powerful red wine.

TECHNICAL DATA

APPELLATION: Napa Valley
COMPOSITION: 91% cabernet sauvignon, 5% merlot, 4% petit verdot
MATURATION: 20 months in 100% French oak barrels
CELLARING: Delicious now, but capable of long-term aging from three to 15-plus years
WEBSITE: www.castellodiamorosa.com

LEARN MORE

Learn more about Castello di Amorosa.

towers, four underground stories, and 95 of its 107 rooms dedicated to winemaking.

Guests come to Castello di Amorosa eager to explore the eight-level Tuscan castle located right in Napa, and they are not disappointed. Dario designed his masterpiece to be replete with all the charming hallmarks expected from any castle: a chapel, a dry moat, a drawbridge, a courtyard, a watch tower, a torture chamber including a Renaissance-era iron maiden, a loggia, an outdoor oven, intentionally bricked-up entrances, and even secret passageways. It's no wonder the castle plays host to a variety of special events, including murder mystery dinners and themed costume parties. Dario also took great care to have the craftsmanship, whether created or sourced, be utterly authentic: thousand-pound hand-hewn doors, hand-painted frescos, ironwork hand-forged by Italian artisans over an open flame, hand-chiseled stones, handmade antique bricks and tile from Europe, and many other distinctive touches that the friendly tour guides are happy to point out and explain. Dario consulted and collaborated extensively over the course of the construction process with numerous architects, builders, artisans, and other craftsmen who shared his passion for medieval architecture. As a result, the

LEFT: After a bountiful harvest, the Primitivo vineyard reveals its fall colors.
Photograph by Jim Sullivan

LA CASTELLANA RESERVE SUPER TUSCAN BLEND NAPA VALLEY

GOURMET PAIRINGS
The elegant Super Tuscan pairs excellently with lamb, sausage, grilled steak, venison, or a great pasta dish such as pappardelle with wild boar. Try it with braised beef in a slightly savory sauce.

TASTING NOTES
Feminine in tone, yet structured, the vibrant red wine shows rich aromatics of pomegranate, fresh red cherry, Tuscan herbs, mocha, wild berry, and currants. Hints of spice and black pepper from the sangiovese mingle with the black cherry lusciousness of the Bordeaux varietals. Elegant and complex, it is balanced with good depth, velvety tannins, and a soft texture.

WINEMAKER'S INSIGHT
Castello di Amorosa wines reflect a balance of Old World style and the terrior of Napa Valley by combining traditional winemaking methods with technologically advanced equipment. Winemaker Brooks Painter optimizes the flavor and varietal components of the grapes by sourcing grapes from various appellations of Napa Valley.

TECHNICAL DATA

APPELLATION: Napa Valley
COMPOSITION: 52% cabernet sauvignon, 27% merlot, 21% sangiovese
MATURATION: 20 months in French oak barrels
CELLARING: Drink now or cellar for three to 15 years
WEBSITE: www.castellodiamorosa.com

LEARN MORE

Learn more about Castello di Amorosa.

BELOW: Dust settles on wine bottles in the cellar.
Photograph by Jim Sullivan

RIGHT: The grand barrel room.
Photograph courtesy of Castello di Amorosa

BOTTOM: At 12,000 square feet, the grand barrel room, replete with its 40 Roman cross-vaults, is constructed from ancient brick imported from Europe.
Photograph by Peter Menzel

FACING PAGE LEFT: *Photograph by Jim Sullivan*
FACING PAGE RIGHT: *Photograph © iStockphoto.com/alle12*

structure is no reproduction: it is a true incarnation of a Tuscan castle, faithful in all respects.

At first, Dario simply wanted to build a small, Tuscan village-style winery and replant the vineyards on the historic site. But as ideas crystallized, he fell in love with the thought of making small lots of primarily Italian-style wines and showcasing them in the castle setting. To ensure quality production of the wines, winemaking did not begin until a decade after the 1994-1996 plantings. Visitors enjoy tasting the expansive portfolio, which includes merlot, cabernet sauvignon, chardonnay, gewürztraminer, sangiovese, pinot grigio, pinot bianco, Muscato Canelli, pinot noir, barbera, primitivo, and special offerings of Rosato di Sangiovese, La Castellana Super Tuscan blend, Il Barone Reserve Cabernet Sauvignon, the popular brachetto-styled

ABOVE LEFT: Dario Sattui and his dog Lupo in the great hall, a magnificent room replete with hand-painted, Italian-style frescos.
Photograph by Rocco Ceselin

TOP: The great hall is dressed and ready for a memorable event.
Photograph by Jim Sullivan

ABOVE: The Knights' Hall is an authentic space, adorned with frescos depicting knights in battle.
Photograph by Peter Menzel

FACING PAGE LEFT: *Photograph © iStockphoto.com/Jancouver*
FACING PAGE RIGHT: *Photograph by Jim Sullivan*

CHARDONNAY RESERVE
BIEN NACIDO VINEYARD

GOURMET PAIRINGS
With its rich flavors and silky texture, this wine pairs exceptionally well with most shellfish including Dungeness crab. Try it with herb-roasted chicken or mild barbecued king salmon.

TASTING NOTES
A dry wine, it suggests aromas of toasted vanilla, melon, and peach, which complement tones of pear and tropical fruit. With a silky texture and hints of toasted nuts, the wine boasts a slightly buttery and oaky bouquet with a lingering finish.

WINEMAKER'S INSIGHT
Our chardonnay is aged sur lie—on the yeast—in French oak barrels for 10 months. Twenty percent of the barrels undergo malolactic fermentation, which softens the acidity and lends a silky texture to the wine.

TECHNICAL DATA

APPELLATION: Santa Maria Valley
COMPOSITION: 100% chardonnay
MATURATION: 10 months in 100% French oak barrels
CELLARING: Cellar for one to five years
WEBSITE: www.castellodiamorosa.com

LEARN MORE

Learn more about Castello di Amorosa.

Caymus Vineyards   RUTHERFORD

The Wagner family's roots run deep in Napa Valley in prune, walnut, and grape farming, and stretch back even further to the grape growing regions of Rheinpfalz, Germany, and Alsace, France. Charlie and Lorna Wagner, skilled home winemakers, entered the professional scene in 1972 with their son Chuck. They established Caymus Vineyards on property purchased in 1941, already in use as the family farm and home. The name Caymus is in tribute to the area which was once known as Rancho Caymus, a former

ABOVE: Beautiful, loose, sun-rich clusters of Wagner-grown cabernet sauvignon grapes.
FACING PAGE: Cabernet vines at sunrise in the Caymus Vineyards Atlas Peak vineyard.
Photographs © Wagner Family of Wine

Mexican land grant.

Charlie and Chuck constructed many of the winery buildings on-site using local materials like Napa Valley stones and wood reclaimed from Liberty School, a one-room schoolhouse on the property that Charlie attended. The focus at Caymus has been on quality and innovation from the start, in both the vineyard and the winery, as well as hands-on techniques. The Wagner family had been winemakers before Prohibition temporarily halted their efforts. The first wines produced under the Caymus label were Johannisberg riesling, pinot noir, and cabernet sauvignon, but soon it was apparent that the Rutherford climate proved best for growing cabernet. Today the cabernet sauvignon grapes are sourced from several specific sub-appellations chosen on the merit of the soil and include both mountain and valley fruit. The estate vineyard surrounds the winery: 60 acres of gravel and clay-loam soil planted to cabernet sauvignon.

ABOVE: It's a hands-on family operation in Califorina with all brands uniting as the Wagner Family of Wine.

FACING PAGE TOP LEFT: Lorna Belle Glos Wagner with son Charles J. "Chuck" Wagner, circa 1974.

FACING PAGE TOP RIGHT: Charles F. "Charlie" Wagner on the farm in Rutherford, circa 1936.

FACING PAGE BOTTOM: Chuck and his father Charlie Wagner building Caymus together, circa 1982.
Photographs © Wagner Family of Wine

Caymus Vineyards' Special Selection was recognized by *Wine Spectator* in 2006 as the most highly-rated Napa Valley cabernet sauvignon across 14 vintages, and lauded by the magazine as the Wine of the Year for both the 1984 and 1990 vintages. The success of Caymus has been acknowledged throughout the world. New generations of the Wagner family continue on a proud family tradition of winemaking.

ABOVE: Winter legumes and mustard plants in the dormant Block A vineyard provide nitrogen to the soil for healthy springtime growth.
Photograph © Wagner Family of Wine

RIGHT: Main entrance to Caymus Vineyards' tasting room and barrel cellar.
Photograph © Wagner Family of Wine

FACING PAGE TOP: Three generations of Wagners: Charlie II, Joseph, Erin, Lorna Belle Glos, Chuck, and Jenny.
Photograph by Tyler Jacobsen

FACING PAGE BOTTOM: Block D is planted specifically to produce greater root competition and higher phenolic concentration in the grapes.
Photograph © Wagner Family of Wine

THIS PAGE: Photograph © Wagner Family of Wine
FACING PAGE LEFT: Photograph © iStockphoto.com/pawelwizja
FACING PAGE RIGHT: Photograph © iStockphoto.com/RiverRockPhotos

NAPA VALLEY CABERNET SAUVIGNON

GOURMET PAIRINGS
The rich flavors of this wine pair deliciously with steak, lasagna, enchiladas, and fettuccine alfredo.

TASTING NOTES
Dark scarlet in color, the nose is sweet fruit and smoked meats. A bouquet of truffle mushrooms and vanilla-style oak gives way to a creamy rich palate with nuances of leather and a cocoa-textured, fine-grain tannin. Flavors of spice, medium toast oak, and cassis create a wine that is fully rich, yet supple.

WINEMAKER'S INSIGHT
Retaining a consistent house character has always been important at Caymus Vineyards; however, Napa Valley has evolved as a unique region by using innovative farming and winemaking practices. Caymus continues along the path of producing exciting and good-tasting Napa Valley wines unlike any other cabernet sauvignons in the world today.

TECHNICAL DATA
APPELLATION: Napa Valley
COMPOSITION: 100% cabernet sauvignon
MATURATION: Aged in extended air-dried 225-liter French oak barrels for 15 to 17 months
CELLARING: Delicious now or cellared; sweet spot is six to eight years from vintage
WEBSITE: www.caymus.com

WATCH A VIDEO

Co-founder Lorna Belle Glos Wagner sits down with her family to reflect on memories of Caymus Vineyards.

SPECIAL SELECTION CABERNET SAUVIGNON

GOURMET PAIRINGS
The wine pairs beautifully with applewood smoked pheasant alongside truffle and parsnip potato gratin, foie gras, fiddleheads prepared with sea salt, and morel mushrooms.

TASTING NOTES
A dark scarlet color with purple edges, the wine expands to a supple juicy character with an intense presence. Flavors of bitter chocolate, charred peppered meat, raw dry-aged beef, brown spice, vanilla, sarsaparilla, and cream soda with judicious grip and texture make an amusing ensemble of harmonies.

WINEMAKER'S INSIGHT
We source the wine's grapes from eight of the 16 Napa Valley sub-appellations: Howell Mountain, Atlas Peak, Oak Knoll, Yountville, Rutherford, St. Helena, Wooden Valley, and Calistoga. The soils are gravelly loam and clay-loam. A balance of two significant components—ripe and abundant tannins and integrated fruit—form the balance of the wine's structure.

TECHNICAL DATA
APPELLATION: Napa Valley
COMPOSITION: 85% cabernet sauvignon, 15% merlot
MATURATION: Aged for 16 months in 25% new French barrels
CELLARING: Delicious now or in 20-plus years; sweet spot is seven to 10 years from vintage
WEBSITE: www.caymus.com

WATCH A VIDEO

Owner and winemaker Chuck Wagner takes a nostalgic look at the 40 years of winemaking at Caymus.

Chappellet Vineyard & Winery   ST. HELENA

Like a modernist flower, the vibrant persimmon-colored pyramid of Chappellet Vineyard & Winery blooms among the verdant trees and vines on the side of Pritchard Hill. When asked by artist Ed Moses what her favorite building was, co-founder Molly Chappellet's answer was the pyramids in Egypt. Thus Chappellet's signature pyramid designed by Ed Moses, which also graces Chappellet wine bottles, was conceived. On the advice of renowned winemaker André Tchelistcheff, Donn and Molly Chappellet solidified their pioneering Napa Valley legacy by becoming the first winery to exclusively plant their vineyards on high-elevation hillsides. It quickly became apparent that the estate vineyards planted on the hill were

ABOVE: The summer dining terrace.

FACING PAGE: From the Chappellet Vineyard, Mount St. Helena can be seen over the Mayacamas Mountain Range.
Photographs by M. J. Wickham

particularly well suited for cabernet sauvignon. Growing at an altitude of 800 to 1,800 feet above sea level, Chappellet's grapes receive a few extra hours of sunshine each day. A variety of contours provide different exposures, creating 34 distinctive blocks along the hillside. Rich deposits of red earth, volcanic rock, clay, gravelly soil, and sandy loam gift Chappellet with wines of varied characteristics. Since its 1967 founding, Chappellet has created sophisticated wines including cabernet sauvignon, cabernet franc, malbec, petit

TOP LEFT: The winery pyramid rises behind cabernet vines.
Photograph courtesy of Chappellet Vineyard & Winery

BOTTOM LEFT: The office entrance to the winery.
Photograph by M. J. Wickham

ABOVE: Donn and Molly Chappellet at the winery entrance.
Photograph by M. J. Wickham

FACING PAGE: *Photographs by M. J. Wickham*

PRITCHARD HILL CABERNET SAUVIGNON

GOURMET PAIRINGS

Lamb is a great complement to cabernet sauvignon; it lets the beauty of the wine shine through. Pair with rack of lamb coated with olive oil, rosemary, balsamic vinegar, and Dijon mustard accompanied by oven-roasted Yukon potatoes.

TASTING NOTES

Pritchard Hill Cabernet Sauvignon represents the pinnacle of Chappellet winemaking. Grown on rocky mountainside vineyards, Chappellet cabernets have consistently displayed an ability to age for several decades. Notes of espresso, dark chocolate, and toasted oak support beautiful ripe fruit and spice flavors with seamless, mouth-coating tannins, adding power and longevity. Despite its epic nature, there is also a liveliness and radiance to the wine that gives it poise, precision, and balance.

WINEMAKER'S INSIGHT

On Pritchard Hill, we're just above the fog line so we do get a cooling effect, but we're in the sun all day. There's always an intensity to the fruit on Pritchard Hill. You don't get high vigor sites up in the hills; you get a lower yield, smaller berries. There's a richness, a bigness, a saturation, but it's never on the herbal side. Most of our wines are 75 to 80-percent cabernet. The rest is petit verdot, malbec, and merlot, varieties with a very different profile.

TECHNICAL DATA

APPELLATION: Napa Valley
COMPOSIT ON: Cabernet sauvignon
MATURATION: 20 months in new French oak
CELLARING: Ages beautifully for 20-plus years, yet enticing to drink on release
WEBSITE: www.chappellet.com

WATCH A VIDEO

Managing director Cyril Chappellet describes the unique growing conditions that contribute to the flavors in Chappellet's Pritchard Hill Cabernet Sauvignon.

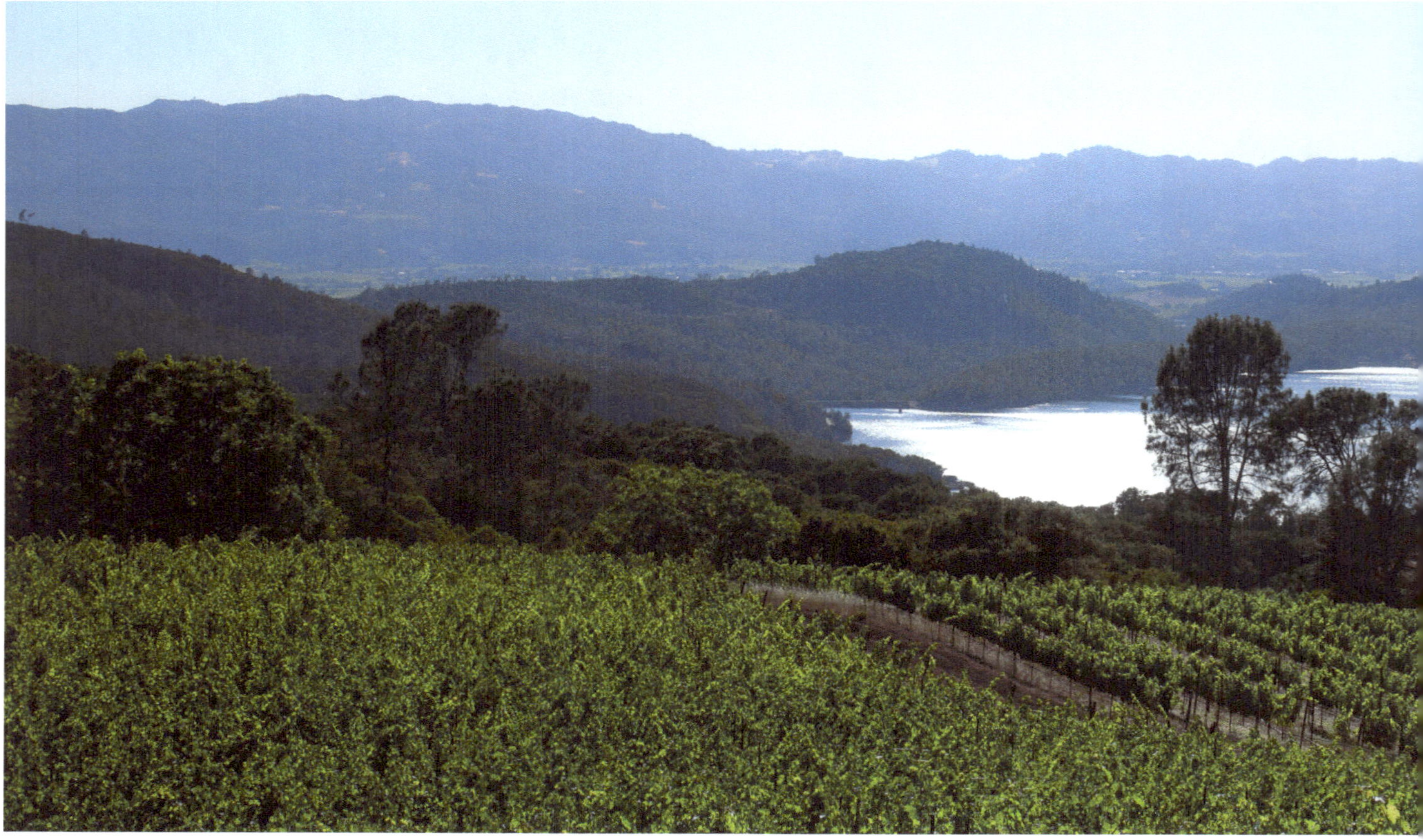

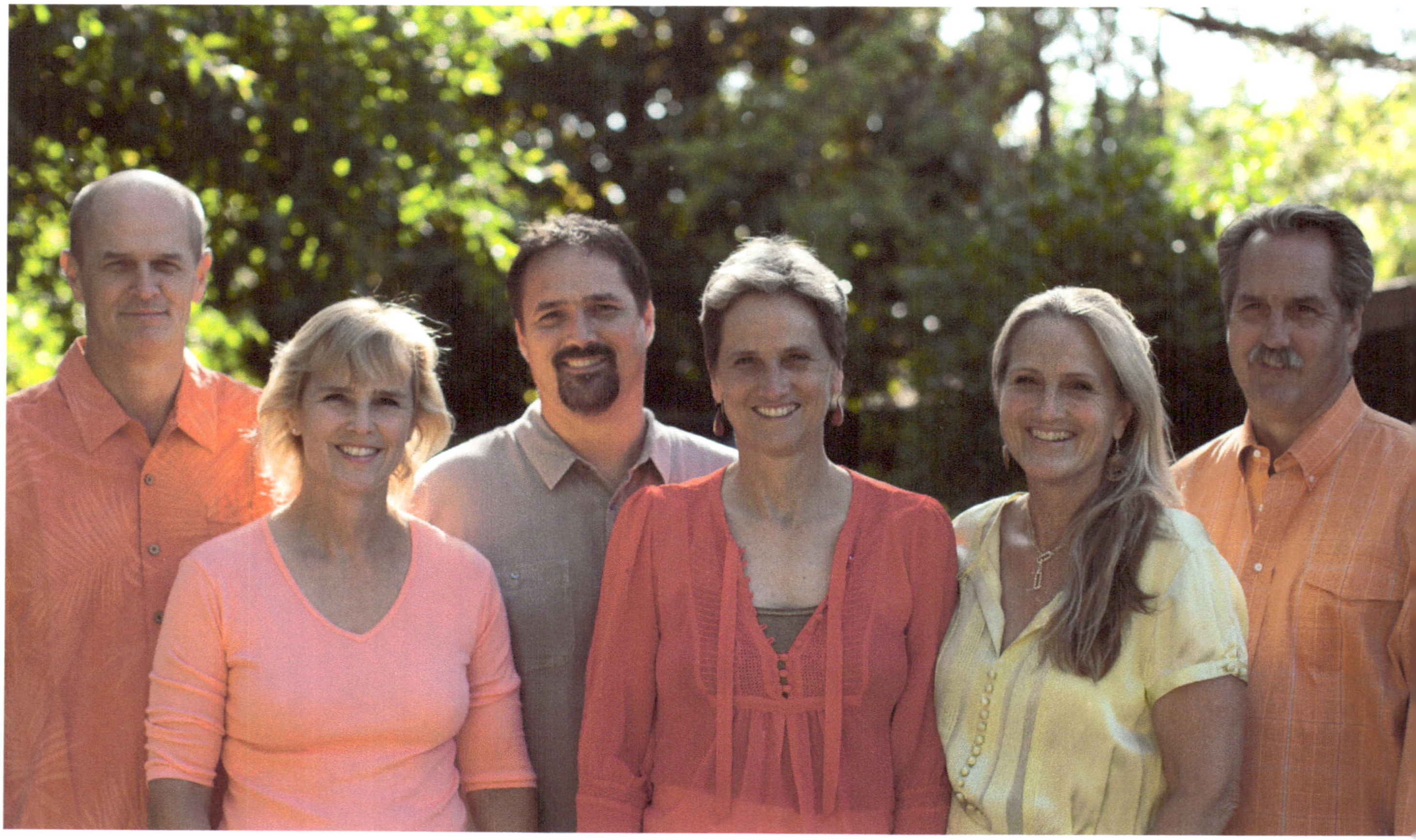

verdot, merlot, petite syrah, zinfandel, chardonnay, and chenin blanc.

At the winery, business is a family affair; all of Donn and Molly's six children are involved in winery operations. Cyril, Carissa, and Jon-Mark serve as managing directors of marketing, legal affairs, and wine and viticulture, respectively. Dominic oversees all audio-visual projects. Their sisters Lygia and Alexa also lend their talents to the company—Lygia provides artwork for the winery and supports marketing in the Monterey area, while Alexa contributes designs for labels and assists with marketing in the Los Angeles area.

Winemaker Phillip Corallo-Titus, vineyard manager David Pirio, and vineyard foreman Enrique Rodriguez have worked together with family members for decades in building the award-winning legacy of Chappellet wines. Among the winery's early claims to fame is a 1969 Jeroboam of Chappellet Cabernet Sauvignon, which sold for the highest price on record for a single bottle of American wine at the first Napa Valley Wine Auction. Recently ranked in the top 30 of the *Wine Spectator*'s Top 100 three years in a row, the 2006 Chappellet Cabernet Sauvignon placed sixth in the world. Chappellet wines have consistently ranked in the 90s, yet it is the focus on the vineyards and family that makes Chappellet an exceptional winery.

LEFT: The west tasting corner in the winery pyramid.
Photograph by M. J. Wickham

FACING PAGE TOP: Lake Hennessey is visible beyond the lower cabernet terraces at dusk.
Photograph by M. J. Wickham

FACING PAGE BOTTOM: Winemaking is a family affair at Chappallet Vineyard & Winery.
Photograph by Guru Khalsa

David Arthur Vineyards ST. HELENA

David Long started making wine when he was in the ninth grade—if winemaking means fermenting apple juice with a nylon sock on the neck of a bottle to keep the flies out. After discovering David's operations in a surprise locker check, the high school principal called him into his office and gave him a good talking to. Little did he know, 20 years later at a high school reunion, David would be standing in front of the same principal with a huge grin and a bottle of David Arthur wine in his hand. Located 1,200 feet above the eastern side of the valley floor in Rutherford, David Arthur Vineyards is the Long family's legacy, started by David's father Don, who became smitten with Napa Valley much in the same way his son would years later.

ABOVE: The winery surrounded by grapevines.
FACING PAGE: The vineyard on Pritchard Hill.
Photographs by M. J. Wickham

At the suggestion of friend André Tchelistcheff, Don slowly acquired over 1,000 acres of land on Pritchard Hill. In 1978, David—immediately hooked on vines—joined his father in clearing the land and planting grapes. Proof that a formal education isn't always the answer, David learned everything he knows about winemaking while scrubbing the tanks at Chappellet Vineyard & Winery, Joseph Phelps Vineyards, and Schramsberg Vineyards. Today winemaker Nile Zacherle and a highly insightful team cultivate small amounts of cabernet sauvignon, cabernet franc, merlot, petite verdot, sangiovese, and nebbiolo.

ABOVE: The barrel room at David Arthur Vineyards.
TOP RIGHT: Guests enjoy many sights when visiting the winery.
RIGHT: David Long and his daughter Laura in the vineyard.
Photographs by M. J. Wickham

FACING PAGE LEFT: *Photograph © iStockphoto.com/ShyMan*
FACING PAGE RIGHT: *Photograph by M. J. Wickham*

ELEVATION 1147

GOURMET PAIRINGS
Beef, duck, and lamb dishes pair best with the wine.

TASTING NOTES
The wine is dark garnet red and nearly opaque with a deep core. The aromas are multi-layered and complex with baked cherries and black currant jam, followed by violets, dark chocolate, and hints of fennel seed and pecans. The texture is sweet with tannin and carries a broad expansive texture with a bold full palate concentration and long finish. The palate finishes with flavors of dark chocolate, espresso bean, baked plums, and boysenberry.

WINEMAKER'S INSIGHT
Our Elevation 1147 always represents the best of the best from David Arthur. The vineyard we source the wine's fruit from sits at an elevation of 1,147 feet above sea level. These few rows of vines have been consistent in their exceptional quality and intriguing flavor profile, inspiring us to bottle the Elevation 1147 as a single-vineyard cabernet sauvignon in a very limited production.

TECHNICAL DATA

APPELLATION: Napa Valley
COMPOSITION: 100% cabernet sauvignon
MATURATION: 23 months in 100% new French oak barrels
CELLARING: Cellar for up to six to 10 years
WEBSITE: www.davidarthur.com

WATCH A VIDEO

Vintner David Long discusses the role the topography of the vineyard plays in producing the winery's flagship wine, Elevation 1147.

Del Dotto Winery ST. HELENA

Just as the name Del Dotto appears in Italian history, that same name has become ubiquitous all over Napa Valley as well. Under the Del Dotto Vineyards umbrella, wine lovers discover three properties dotting the Northern California landscape: Del Dotto Historic Winery and Caves in Napa, and Del Dotto Venetian Estate Winery and Caves and sister label Villa Del Lago Winery, both in St. Helena. The Del Dotto family has established itself as one in Napa's first families, just as its ancestors were in Venice. Del Dotto Vineyards aims to harness both ancient and modern winemaking

ABOVE: Front of the Venetian Estate Winery.
FACING PAGE: The view of Del Dotto's backyard from the private wine cellar.
Photographs by M. J. Wickham

THE DAVID

GOURMET PAIRINGS
For a sublime experience, pair with Eden Farms pork loin wrapped in house-cured pancetta, morel mushroom sformato, sweet carrot fonduta, California Delta asparagus, and Madras curry gastrique.

TASTING NOTES
Characteristic of the wine is a sense of ripe, extracted fruit, and balanced flavors with silky tannins. Blueberries and black cherries weave together with cinnamon, nutmeg, and white pepper on the palate. Sexy and sophisticated, The David continues to sing with light overtones of Rutherford dust, bittersweet chocolate, and espresso.

WINEMAKER'S INSIGHT
The grapes, picked at the peak of ripeness and flavor development, come to the winery early in the morning for a meticulous pre-sorting, de-stemming, and post-sorting process. In a fermenter, they cold soak at 50 degrees to extract flavor and color. The juices drained after fermenting age in oak for a total of 12 months before varietal blending occurs, then age again before bottling.

TECHNICAL DATA

APPELLATION: Rutherford
COMPOSITION: Cabernet sauvignon, merlot, cabernet franc
MATURATION: Five days' cold soak, 10 days in fermenter, 100% free run
CELLARING: Enjoy now and for years to come
WEBSITE: www.deldottovineyards.com

WATCH A VIDEO

President David Del Dotto goes into the making of The David, a classic Bordeaux blend.

techniques to produce great wines to enjoy with family and friends.

Venice, Italy, 1103: The Del Dotto family was one of 500 that held power in governing the city. Carignano, Tuscany, 1450: The family began to make red wine. Merced, California, late 1800s: Dominic Del Dotto moved to the New World, bringing with him Old World traditions. Dominic's youngest son, John, observed his father's winemaking efforts and instilled a love of wine in his son, David. Finally, in 1988, David and his wife Yolanda purchased land in St. Helena. By 1990, he'd planted cabernet sauvignon, cabernet franc, merlot, and sangiovese; *Wine Spectator* rated the debut 1993 cabernet sauvignon an astonishing 92 points. In 1997, the family brought Nils Venge on as consulting winemaker and expanded production from 500 to 5,000

TOP: The tasting area at the Venetian Estate Winery.

ABOVE: VIP Grand Wine and Food pairing lounge at the Estate Venetian Winery.

LEFT: David and Yolanda Del Dotto.
Photographs by M. J. Wickham

FACING PAGE: *Photographs by M. J. Wickham*

cases. Almost right from the start, Del Dotto Vineyards' growth exploded into a stellar reputation that has held firm ever since.

2006 saw another burst of activity: When Gerard Zanzonico came on board as winemaker, wine ratings skyrocketed to the mid-90s and the St. Helena Venetian Estate Winery and Caves opened. Reflecting ancient Venetians' desire to live in a beautiful world, the design incorporates Italian marble walls, tiles depicting the history of wine, Venetian crystal chandeliers, gold-inlaid ceilings, and mosaic marble floors. The original Napa estate and winery also contains caves, hand-dug in 1885 but restored and opened in 1999. A Del Dotto hallmark is bottling wine directly from oak barrels; the winemakers love the flavors imparted by the wood and experiment with domestic and international barrels. Both sets of caves are an excellent place to taste Del Dotto wines and undergo barrel-tasting.

TOP: Vineyard 887 in the St. Helena appellation.

BOTTOM: Entrance to back of the caves at the Venetian Estate Winery.

FACING PAGE: The Venetian Estate Cave features 300-year-old terracotta ceiling tiles, 18th-century-style hand-blown Murano chandeliers, five-color hand-cut Viareggio marble walls, and stone floors inlaid with Verona marble, modeled after the Doges Palace walkway in Venice.
Photographs by M. J. Wickham

Today the winery produces 12,000 cases of cave-aged wine that draw on the chardonnay, pinot noir, cabernet sauvignon, cabernet franc, merlot, and sangiovese organically farmed on 120 acres spread across seven vineyards. Always in search of what will make the greatest wine imaginable, the Del Dotto team's pioneer spirit keeps it on top in Napa Valley.

ABOVE: Del Dotto's private wine cellar.

LEFT: The Del Dotto private salumi room, with handmade salumi by Del Dotto's private chefs.
Photographs by M. J. Wickham

FACING PAGE: *Photographs by M. J. Wickham*

VILLA DEL LAGO CABERNET SAUVIGNON

GOURMET PAIRINGS

Our chef advises a pairing with glazed Meyer Ranch beef short rib, accented by English peas, cipollini onions, shaved radish, and pea tendril salad, topped with Périgord truffle jus.

TASTING NOTES

From the beginning of its beautiful mouthfeel to the long, silky finish, the wine shows not only the beautiful and lush mountain dark fruits but also caramelized sugar and chocolate flavors reminiscent of the finest blend of handmade French oak barrels made by artisans. The concentrated flavor also displays plum, mushroom, and cassis notes.

WINEMAKER'S INSIGHT

The vineyard, farmed organically, is ground-seeded with cover crop and mowed in spring. A green harvest in early June precedes bunch thinning and de-leafing in September, then manual picking and grape sorting before and after de-stemming. Only whole berries are put in tanks.

TECHNICAL DATA

APPELLATION: Napa Valley
COMPOSITION: 100% cabernet sauvignon
MATURATION: Five days' cold soak, 10 days in fermenter, 100% free run
CELLARING: Enjoy now and for years to come
WEBSITE: www.deldottovineyards.com

LEARN MORE

Learn more about Del Dotto Winery.

Domaine Carneros NAPA

France's champagne industry is legendary, but it was Claude Taittinger's genius idea to bring the tradition of sparkling wine to California's cool Carneros appellation. In the late 1970s, Taittinger of Champagne Taittinger proclaimed that world-class sparkling wine could be produced in America and founded the perfect location in the heart of Carneros. Domaine Carneros was established in 1987 with Eileen Crane at the helm. She remains the winery's CEO and founding winemaker, renowned throughout the wine world for her skill, leadership, and natural charm.

ABOVE: Domaine Carneros' estate-grown organic vineyards. The Carneros appellation provides the ideal micro-climate for growing chardonnay and pinot noir grapes.
Photograph by Curt Fischer

FACING PAGE: The Domaine Carneros château is a Wine Country landmark, architecturally inspired by the Taittinger-owned 18th-century Château de la Marquetterie in Champagne, France.
Photograph by M. J. Wickham

Widely recognized as one of California's finest producers, Domaine Carneros' impressive portfolio features sparkling wines noted for their elegant yet intense style, and balanced, complex pinot noirs crafted by TJ Evans, the winery's pinot noir winemaker. Sparkling wine notables include the popular Domaine Carneros Vintage Brut Cuvée, Domaine Carneros Brut Rosé, and Le Rêve Blanc de Blancs. Pinot noir lovers have long admired the winery's estate bottling and, for special occasions, The Famous Gate—a wine crafted in very limited quantities. In fact, all of Domaine Carneros' wines are produced in limited quantities; fruit comes almost exclusively from the winery's certified organic estate vineyards. The winery's commitment to quality is evident at the spectacular château in Carneros and in each bottle.

TOP: Situated atop a knoll surrounded by organic estate vineyards, the winery château is a regional landmark, with expansive outdoor terraces and breathtaking views of vineyard-covered hills.
Photograph by M. J. Wickham

MIDDLE: The Taittinger family of Champagne Taittinger selected Eileen Crane, CEO and founding winemaker, to oversee the planning and development of the winery and vineyards.
Photograph courtesy of Domaine Carneros

BOTTOM: Known for its hospitality, the winery offers table service on the terrace or in the salon, with a delightful wine and food pairing menu.
Photograph by M. J. Wickham

FACING PAGE: *Photographs by M. J. Wickham*

LE RÊVE BLANC DE BLANCS

GOURMET PAIRINGS

A luxurious sparkling cuvée, Le Rêve is an inspired selection for great moments. Savor it with caviar, shellfish, smoked fish, poultry, goat cheese, and double- or triple-cream cheeses and fresh fruit.

TASTING NOTES

Alluring aromas of white flowers, stone fruit, honeysuckle, pear, fig, lime, and yeasty brioche make for a seductive overture. The wine's rich, round palate, with its layers of white fruit, crème brûlée, and toasted almond flavors, lingers through an extraordinarily long, silky finish.

WINEMAKER'S INSIGHT

Le Rêve, French for "the dream," is Domaine Carneros's Tête de Cuvée—the pinnacle of our sparkling wine portfolio. Repeatedly honored as America's best, it is a sophisticated wine of exceptional finesse, typically crafted from several distinct clones of 100-percent certified-organic, estate-grown chardonnay. A pure expression of our Carneros estate vineyards, it is produced in extremely limited quantities.

TECHNICAL DATA

APPELLATION: Carneros
COMPOSITION: Five distinct clones of certified-organic estate-grown chardonnay
MATURATION: Aged in the bottle, on the lees, for five and a half years
CELLARING: Exquisite upon release, it will continue developing complexity for years to come
WEBSITE: www.domainecarneros.com

LEARN MORE

Learn more about Domaine Carneros.

Fantesca Estate & Winery   ST. HELENA

La Fantesca graced the stages of Italian improvisational theater in the 16th century; she was a witty, sexy woman in a male-dominated art: young, clever, and adventurous. With a nod to this fun spirit, Fantesca Estate & Winery owners Susan and Duane Hoff approach winemaking seriously, but always with an emphasis on what's important in life: family, friends, food, and of course, wine. The Minneapolis natives fell in love with Napa Valley over several romantic rendezvous and decided to change careers, exchanging the busy urban corporate world for the idyllic setting of Napa's rolling hills and foggy vineyards.

ABOVE: Fewer than 800 cases of Fantesca Estate Cabernet Sauvignon are produced annually.

FACING PAGE: Reclaimed after Prohibition and replanted in 1997, Fantesca's vineyard sprawls over 10 acres of steep mountainside, producing a shallow bowl that is just right for growing a robust cabernet.
Photographs by M. J. Wickham

FANTESCA'S ALL GREAT THINGS: FREEDOM

GOURMET PAIRINGS
For a unique main course, pair with roasted duck topped with crushed pistachios, medjool dates, and coffee jus as created by Michelin Star Chef Brandon Sharp of SolBar.

TASTING NOTES
Deep ruby in color, the wine boasts aromas of warm, ripe fruit and an earthiness that can't be missed. Complex and layered with explosive bright berry flavor, completely mouth-coating with an impression of dense, sweet, candy-like fruit, the wine is sure to delight with its moderate, refined tannins and persistent flavors.

WINEMAKER'S INSIGHT
This unique and special blend is inspired by Sir Winston Churchill, who said that all great things are simple enough to be expressed in one word, freedom being the first. By releasing All Great Things constrained only as a "Napa Valley red wine," famed winemaker Heidi Peterson Barrett has the opportunity to select any varietal from any vineyard within Napa Valley to create this delicious vintage. It truly is a winemaker's wine.

TECHNICAL DATA

APPELLATION: Napa Valley
COMPOSITION: Proprietary red blend of noble grape varieties
MATURATION: 18 months in French oak barrels
CELLARING: Exquisite upon release; ages nicely for 10 to 15 years
WEBSITE: www.fantesca.com

WATCH A VIDEO

Proprietor Duane Hoff describes winemaker Heidi Barrett's unique creation, Fantesca's All Great Things.

Their vineyard was originally part of Caroline Bale's dowry when she married Charles Krug in 1860, and from that point through today Fantesca has become a legacy rich in feminine influence, like its namesake. Today the winery employs the winemaking expertise of Heidi Barrett, the valley's "First Lady of Wine," also called the "Queen of Cult Cabernet" by Robert Parker Jr. But it was the Hoffs' dream that returned this spirited

TOP: On a garden stroll, proprietors Susan and Duane Hoff ponder what to pick for dinner over a glass of All Great Things.

ABOVE: The Hoffs' rose gardens are delightful to both the eye and the nose.

LEFT: Wine tasting overlooking the vineyard captivates visitors, no matter the season.
Photographs by M. J. Wickham

FACING PAGE: *Photographs by M. J. Wickham*

wine production to the estate.

Located on the southeastern side of Spring Mountain, the vineyard plantings benefit from tremendous variation in slope among the 10 acres of vines. The elevation and mountain terrain offer excellent sun exposure and a long grape growing season. A team led by Jim Barbour manages the mountain vines, which produce rich, intense cabernet. Together with the Hoffs, the Fantesca winemaking team possesses a spirit of pride. A sense of ownership permeates the enterprise, accentuated with a love for the Napa Valley lifestyle; the Hoffs are truly living the American dream.

ABOVE: Fantesca's caves penetrate 297 feet through the mountain range. The caves are rumored to be an abandoned silver mine.
Photograph by Leigh Hagen, LHGFX

LEFT: Fantesca's private tasting room provides an elegant environment to experience its highly acclaimed wines.
Photograph by M. J. Wickham

FACING PAGE: *Photographs by M. J. Wickham*

ESTATE CABERNET SAUVIGNON

GOURMET PAIRINGS
For a wonderful dinner, pair a cowboy steak with pickled chanterelles, chimichurri, and giant duck fat fries as created by Michelin Star Chef Brandon Sharp of SolBar.

TASTING NOTES
Garnet red in color, the cabernet sauvignon possesses aromas of ripe blackberry, black cherry, cedar, spice, toasty French oak, and a hint of cinnamon. Across the palate, the flavors are similar to the nose; ripe fruit dominates with a more subtle touch of oak. The wine is silky in the mouth, with velvety soft, balanced, and well-behaved tannins.

WINEMAKER'S INSIGHT
Grapes from Spring Mountain produce wines with beautiful acid balance, length, and a refinement that pairs excellently with a variety of cuisine. The wine cellars well and may be enjoyed for years after bottling.

TECHNICAL DATA

APPELLATION: Spring Mountain District
COMPOSITION: Vintage dependent, an estate blend of cabernet sauvignon and petite verdot
MATURATION: 18 months in French oak barrels
CELLARING: Exquisite upon release; ages nicely for 15 to 20 years
WEBSITE: www.fantesca.com

WATCH A VIDEO

Proprietress Susan Hoff presents the Fantesca Estate Cabernet Sauvignon as an expression of Napa Valley mountain fruit.

Frog's Leap   RUTHERFORD

Frog's Leap was founded by the Williams family in 1981 on a spot along Mill Creek known as the Frog Farm. An old ledger revealed that around the turn of the century, frogs were raised on the property and sold, no doubt, to enhance the tables of Victorian San Francisco gourmands. Today Frog's Leap makes its home amongst 130 acres of vineyards in Rutherford at the historic Red Barn, built in 1884 as part of the Adamson Winery. Winemakers John Williams and Paula Moschetti handcraft annual productions of sauvignon blanc, chardonnay, zinfandel, merlot, and cabernet sauvignon,

ABOVE: The Red Barn at Frog's Leap.
Photograph by Thomas Heinser

FACING PAGE: Rossi Vineyard in Rutherford.
Photograph by Peter Bowers

all of which are organically grown and made using traditional methods.

Reflecting the belief that quality vines produce quality fruit, Frog's Leap dry-farms over 200 acres of certified organic vineyards. The process requires a deeper root structure, but results in fruit with greater balance and vines that are stronger and more disease-resistant. The grapes are harvested at their natural ripeness, making use of the subtle character and flavors of the fruit that are not overpowered by alcohol when processed.

With an eye toward environmental stewardship, Frog's Leap's sustainability extends to all parts of the winery. Since 2005, it has been powered by 1,020 photovoltaic panels and boasts the first LEED certified hospitality center and administrative office in Napa Valley.

ABOVE LEFT: The interior of the barrel chai.
TOP: John Williams, owner and winemaker.
ABOVE: The vineyard house.
Photographs by Thomas Heinser

FACING PAGE LEFT: *Photograph © iStockphoto.com/LauriPatterson*
FACING PAGE RIGHT: *Photograph by Peter Bowers*

FROG'S LEAP CABERNET SAUVIGNON

GOURMET PAIRINGS
The wine pairs exquisitely with wild mushroom ravioli in a porcini broth, risotto with wild mushrooms and broccoli rabe, or simply grilled lamb chops.

TASTING NOTES
The cabernet boasts flavors of rich red and purple fruits—ripe plums, elderberries, and ruby red cherries—with supple tannins and a lovely acidity.

WINEMAKER'S INSIGHT
Napa Valley is perfectly suited to grow great cabernet. Rather than make the pick-late, sweet-fruit, high-alcohol wines that are now popular, we learned from the past, favoring the lessons passed on by Tchelistcheff, Daniel, and others. Our attempt is not to emulate anyone, but rather to avoid sacrificing the balance between the cabernet's ripe fruit character and its lean, earthy side.

TECHNICAL DATA
APPELLATION: Napa Valley
COMPOSITION: Cabernet sauvignon, cabernet franc, merlot; percentages vary with vintage
MATURATION: 21 months in French oak
CELLARING: Cellar for eight to 10 years
WEBSITE: www.frogsleap.com

LEARN MORE

Learn more about Frog's Leap.

Gargiulo Vineyards   OAKVILLE

Gargiulo Vineyards, recognized as one of Napa Valley's most collectible cabernet sauvignon producers, began as the dream of Jeff and Valerie Gargiulo. A lifelong farmer, Jeff knew he must start with extraordinary land to achieve his vision for a premier wine estate. Luckily Valerie's cousins and Napa grape growing pioneers Barney and Belle Rhodes of Bella Oaks Vineyard were there to help. After much advice from the Rhodes and years of looking for the perfect properties, Jeff and Valerie purchased their first vineyard in 1992: Money Road Ranch, in the heart of Oakville. Eight years later they added a second vineyard, 575 OVX, found in Oakville's red, rocky eastern hills. Since that auspicious beginning, Gargiulo Vineyards has gained recognition as one of Napa Valley's first-growth wine estates.

ABOVE: In addition to fine wine, Jeff Gargiulo is also passionate about music. Performances from Grammy Award-winning artists are held throughout the year on the stage at 575 OVX with the Mayacama Mountains in the distance.
Photograph courtesy of Sue Negrini

FACING PAGE: In the early 1800s, the property was part of George C. Yount's hunting grounds. The water tower now houses the Gargiulo's library vintages going back to 1999.
Photograph by M. J. Wickham

Jeff and Valerie continue to preside as founders and the winery's worldwide ambassadors, while their daughter April acts as brand director. The family's winemaking philosophy favors a gentle and patient approach to protect the grapes' delicate flavors and aromas. Using small, open-top French oak barrels, the Gargiulo winemaking team separately ferments up to 40 individual vineyard blocks to preserve the distinctiveness of each lot. The final blend of these blocks always provides the most vivid expression of the vineyard, varietal, and vintage. Hand-harvesting before dawn, hand-sorting the grapes three times, and processing the wine at the state-of-the-art gravity-flow winery are other ways the Gargiulo team ensures the most expressive wines. With a production total of 4,500 cases, the winery focuses on four wines: Money Road Ranch Cabernet Sauvignon, G Major 7 Cabernet Sauvignon, 575 OVX Cabernet Sauvignon, and Aprile Super Oakville Blend. The prime Oakville vineyard locations and the Gargiulo family's passion combine to make wines that collectors and wine lovers alike hold in the highest regard.

TOP: The Money Road Ranch vineyard's terroir is strikingly different than the OVX vineyard. Its deep loam soil creates wine with Oakville's classic dark and brooding fruit profile.
Photograph by Stefano Massei

MIDDLE: Gargiulo's two Oakville vineyards, Money Road Ranch on left and 575 OVX on right, are only one mile apart, yet each enjoys distinct soil composition. The distinct soils create the vineyards' unique wine characteristics.
Photograph by Stefano Massei

BOTTOM: The Gargiulos practice sustainable agriculture and bring that philosophy to the winery's design. The tasting room was built from repurposed materials: a basketball court floor, a barrel chandelier, and rock walls quarried from the vineyard below.
Photograph by M. J. Wickham

FACING PAGE: Proprietor Jeff Gargiulo walks amongst the vines at 575 OVX vineyard. The distinctive red color comes from iron in the soil and is unique to eastern Oakville.
Photograph courtesy of Paul Dyer

THIS PAGE: *Photograph by M. J. Wickham*

MONEY ROAD RANCH CABERNET SAUVIGNON

TASTING NOTES

The wine's aromas of dark berries, black cherry, slate, mocha, and even tobacco point to its classic Oakville character, a region put on the map as Napa Valley's most sought-after cabernet sauvignon destination. The palate is rich and complex with seamlessly integrated layers of brooding dark fruit and refined tannins.

WINEMAKER'S INSIGHT

Money Road Ranch sits in the heart of Oakville and enjoys optimal daily oscillating temperatures of 35 degrees Fahrenheit or more. That swing elongates the growing season, which allows for the vineyard's hallmark brooding flavors to develop in the wine. In addition, the deep, gravelly loam soil was part of an ancient alluvial fan, which adds to the distinct richness and earthiness found in Money Road Ranch Cabernet Sauvignon.

TECHNICAL DATA

APPELLATION: Oakville
COMPOSITION: 100% cabernet sauvignon
MATURATION: Aged for 20 months in medium toast 90% new French oak
CELLARING: Developing for at least 20 years
WEBSITE: www.gargiulovineyards.com

575 OVX CABERNET SAUVIGNON

TASTING NOTES

The most striking characteristic may be the elegance and balance that such a concentrated and powerful wine can achieve. The nose reveals delicate aromas of rose petal and red berries, which on the palate become lush fruit flavors complemented by a unique, exotic minerality. The last sip in the glass is the most treasured, as it has only just begun to reveal its complexity of flavors.

WINEMAKER'S INSIGHT

Our most limited-release cabernet sauvignon, 575 OVX is produced in quantities of fewer than 300 cases per year. It is devoted to the pure and true expression of a single vineyard in a single vintage. Grapes for the 575 OVX Cabernet Sauvignon are hand-chosen at dawn from our western and southern exposure hillside blocks to express the distinct red rock terroir of the 575 OVX vineyard.

TECHNICAL DATA

APPELLATION: Oakville
COMPOSITION: 100% cabernet sauvignon
MATURATION: Aged for 22 months in medium toast 100% new French oak
CELLARING: Developing for at least 25 years
WEBSITE: www.gargiulovineyards.com

G MAJOR 7 CABERNET SAUVIGNON

TASTING NOTES

The nose reflects subtle floral notes such as rose petal and geranium, which develop into deep and intoxicating crushed berry and mineral earth flavors on the palate. Its tannins are refined and seamlessly integrated. The wine is highly nuanced and provides a profound sense of elegance and complexity, changing with every swirl and sip.

WINEMAKER'S INSIGHT

A blend of select fruit from the 575 OVX vineyard, G Major 7 is named after the classic jazz guitar chord. Like its namesake, it is composed of four notes, or in this case classic Bordeaux grape varietals: cabernet sauvignon, cabernet franc, petit verdot, and merlot. G Major 7 is our only cabernet sauvignon blend and as such we seek to create the most harmonious wine possible with each vintage.

TECHNICAL DATA

APPELLATION: Oakville
COMPOSITION: 85% cabernet sauvignon; 12% cabernet franc, 2% petit verdot, 1% merlot
MATURATION: Aged for 22 months in medium toast 90% new French oak
CELLARING: Developing for at least 20 years
WEBSITE: www.gargiulovineyards.com

WATCH A VIDEO

Vintner Jeff Gargiulo demonstrates how Gargiulo's vineyard practices and blending techniques come together in harmony like music.

Grgich Hills Estate RUTHERFORD

The name Grgich first attracted worldwide attention when Miljenko "Mike" Grgich's Chateau Montelena chardonnay won out over France's best at the famed 1976 Judgment of Paris. The blind tasting revolutionized the wine industry the world over, and also allowed Mike to partner with Austin Hills of Hills Bros. Coffee in 1977 and found Grgich Hills Cellar. Wine lovers flocked to Mike's home base, eager to taste the wine that had changed everything. In 2007, the name changed to Grgich Hills Estate, reflecting the decision to use only grapes from estate vineyards starting with the 2003 vintage.

ABOVE: The demonstration vineyard in front of Grgich Hills Estate introduces visitors to all the grape varieties that the winery grows.

FACING PAGE: Miljenko "Mike" Grgich's home overlooks the vineyard above Calistoga, one of five estate vineyards.
Photographs by M. J. Wickham

CHARDONNAY

GOURMET PAIRINGS
Showcase the wine's elegance with fresh seafood, roasted chicken, grilled pork, or creamy cheeses.

TASTING NOTES
Following the classic style that winemaker Mike Grgich followed upon establishing Grgich Hills in 1977, the chardonnay does not undergo malolactic fermentation. Biodynamic farming creates a wine alive with delicious acidity. The fragrant chardonnay is rich with aromas of ripe peach, mango, and tropical flowers, plus a note of minerality.

WINEMAKER'S INSIGHT
The chardonnay grows in our American Canyon and Carneros vineyards in the southern tip of Napa Valley, not far from San Pablo Bay, which spills into the San Francisco Bay. The cool maritime breezes and fog allow the grapes to slowly ripen to develop complex flavors while maintaining a pleasing natural acidity that is impossible to achieve in warmer areas. All vineyards are certified organic and biodynamic.

TECHNICAL DATA

APPELLATION: Napa Valley
COMPOSITION: 100% chardonnay
MATURATION: Fermented, aged 10 months in 60% neutral, 40% new French oak barrels
CELLARING: Peaks at seven to 10 years from vintage date, can cellar for 20
WEBSITE: www.grgich.com

WATCH A VIDEO

Co-proprietor Violet Grgich talks about the winery's role in ushering in the Napa Valley chardonnay revolution.

Mike hails from Croatia, where he grew up drinking wine and stomping grapes and pursued a straightforward, thorough study of winemaking and viticulture before moving to Napa in 1958. He studied with André Tchelistcheff and worked at Robert Mondavi Winery, then Chateau Montelena, where he crafted that legendary chardonnay. Mike's pedigree and experience alone explain that initial meteoric success, but the secret to what has also sustained the winery ever since lies in its commitment to natural winemaking. Committed to sustainability, the winery farms 366 acres across five estate vineyards without artificial pesticides or herbicides and has run on solar power since 2006.

TOP: Cabernet sauvignon vines surround the winery.

LEFT: The fountain in the olive grove in front of the winery features the Croatian crest, honoring Mike Grgich's homeland, and a rearing horse clenching a baton in its mouth, a colorful feature of the Hills family crest.

RIGHT: Mike Grgich at his home overlooking his Calistoga vineyard.
Photographs by M. J. Wickham

FACING PAGE: *Photographs by M. J. Wickham*

Deliberately keeping the size small—70,000 cases a year—allows the team of Mike, daughter Violet, and nephew Ivo Jeramez to focus on quality above all. While Violet manages the business aspects, Ivo oversees the vineyards and wine production. As one of the wineries to first put the region on the map, Grgich now enjoys international recognition as a benchmark for Napa Valley. In addition to world-class chardonnays like the one that won over France, Grgich produces fumé blanc, zinfandel, cabernet sauvignon, merlot, and a dessert wine named Violetta, after Violet Grgich. The team crafts wines with quality, consistency, and longevity in mind, seeking vintages that possess food-friendly, balanced, and elegant qualities.

TOP: Mike's daughter Violet Grgich often greets visitors at the winery.

MIDDLE: The olive grove in front of the winery is the perfect place for a private lunch, dinner, or tasting.

BOTTOM: The VIP room offers private seated tastings, including library wines, plus pairings with cheese or chocolate.
Photographs by M. J. Wickham

FACING PAGE: *Photographs by M. J. Wickham*

NAPA VALLEY CABERNET SAUVIGNON

GOURMET PAIRINGS
Velvety smooth, it's the perfect partner to grilled steak, rack of lamb, or roasted duck.

TASTING NOTES
The cabernet sauvignon is an elegant wine with rich aromas of blackberries, black licorice, and a hint of cocoa powder. Fermenting using only yeasts that naturally occur on the grapes allows the wine to gain flavors and color from extended skin contact. Each lot is aged separately for several months, and then blended to create a wine that is more complex than the individual parts.

WINEMAKER'S INSIGHT
The Yountville vineyard provides the heart of the Napa Valley Cabernet Sauvignon, with the Rutherford and Calistoga vineyards rounding out the blend. All vineyards are certified organic and biodynamic. The result is a full-bodied, elegant cabernet sauvignon with pure flavors and a pronounced sense of place.

TECHNICAL DATA
APPELLATION: Napa Valley
COMPOSITION: 88% cabernet sauvignon, 5% petit verdot, 3% merlot, 4% cabernet franc
MATURATION: Aged for 21 months in 60% new French oak
CELLARING: Peaks at around 10 years, can cellar for up to 20 to 30 years
WEBSITE: www.grgich.com

WATCH A VIDEO

Vice president of vineyards and production Ivo Jeramez describes what makes Grgich Hills Estate's Napa Valley Cabernet Sauvignon an excellent wine.

Heitz Wine Cellars ST. HELENA

Heitz Wine Cellars' impeccable reputation for quality has contributed to the international stature of Napa Valley since 1961, when Joe and Alice Heitz founded the family winery. Joe's genius for winemaking and his bold ideas helped to usher in a new era; he believed that Napa Valley deserved a place on the world stage as one of the premier winemaking regions. He worked to make that vision a reality by setting unparalleled standards for his wines which brought worldwide attention to Napa Valley.

ABOVE: As committed stewards of the land, the Heitz family practices sustainable farming at all the vineyards, the majority of which are now certified organic.
Photograph by Mark Neal

FACING PAGE: The historic cellar, constructed in 1898 of hand-chiseled stone.
Photograph by Robert Holmes

MARTHA'S VINEYARD CABERNET SAUVIGNON

GOURMET PAIRINGS
For a delicious classic, pair the wine with tender, oven-roasted rack of lamb glazed with honey mustard and accompanied by crisp haricots verts.

TASTING NOTES
Pure and concentrated, the wine's lush varietal aroma reveals the celebrated beauty of its unique Napa Valley terroir. It is a well-integrated cabernet with a generous core of dark, rich fruit that is lightly embraced with mint. Wonderfully complex layers of black cherry flavor unfold with elegance on the palate, building to a long, lovely finish.

WINEMAKER'S INSIGHT
Situated on a lush alluvial plain at the base of the Mayacamas foothills, Martha's Vineyard basks in the morning sun, cooling down earlier than the valley floor. Owned by the May family, this vineyard is home to a proprietary cabernet clone famed for its splendid concentration of flavor. In 1966, the Heitz family formed a historic bond with the Mays, which continues today, to produce wine from this exquisite fruit.

TECHNICAL DATA

APPELLATION: Oakville
COMPOSITION: 100% cabernet sauvignon
MATURATION: One year in American oak; two and a half in Limousin barrels
CELLARING: Certain to impress today; graceful aging ensured for 15 years or more
WEBSITE: www.heitzcellar.com

WATCH A VIDEO

President Kathleen Heitz Myers discusses the complexity of Heitz Wine Cellars' Martha's Vineyard Cabernet Sauvignon, Napa's first vineyard-designated cabernet.

For two generations, the Heitz family has produced a dazzling portfolio of wines, highlighted by their universally acclaimed cabernet sauvignons. Chardonnay, sauvignon blanc, grignolino, zinfandel, and port are crafted specifically for sharing around the table with family and friends. All wines are classic in style, reflecting a calculated restraint that allows for appreciation of the true character of each varietal.

Heitz Cellars cabernet sauvignons have long been celebrated for their purity of flavor and proven record of ageability. They are allowed to mature at an uncommonly slow pace, underscoring the family's view that it takes time to produce cabernets that are balanced and well-integrated. The Martha's Vineyard Cabernet Sauvignon has impressed connoisseurs since 1966, when it became the first Napa cabernet with a vineyard designation on the label. Along with the excellent Trailside Vineyard Cabernet Sauvignon, both collectible wines can be found in distinguished cellars around the world.

TOP: President Kathleen Heitz Myers and winemaker David Heitz are the second generation to lead the family winery.

BOTTOM: A wine press from an earlier era sits near the stone cellar. *Photographs by M. J. Wickham*

FACING PAGE LEFT: *Photograph by M. J. Wickham*
FACING PAGE RIGHT: *Photograph courtesy of Heitz Wine Cellars*

The heart of the Heitz winemaking facility is a historic cellar, constructed of hand-chiseled stone in 1898. Tucked into the eastern hills of St. Helena and surrounded by pristine farmland, this property is part of an agricultural operation that includes a marvelous diversity of acreage throughout the Napa Valley. As committed stewards of the land, the Heitz family practices sustainable farming in all of the vineyards; the majority are now certified organic. They also donated several acres to the Land Trust of Napa County to be used as a conservation easement for the benefit of future generations.

LEFT: The May family owns Martha's Vineyard. The Heitz family has produced legendary wine from that fruit since the first harvest in 1966.
Photograph by M. J. Wickham

The Heitz brand is flourishing with second-generation siblings Kathleen Heitz Myers and David Heitz as president and winemaker. They have continued to safeguard the traditions that make Heitz wines memorable while incorporating technology and new ideas into the family business. Today the Heitz Cellars label is recognized globally as a symbol of fine wine, and the family legacy of quality and integrity is also the vision for the third generation.

ABOVE: At the Heitz Wine Cellars sales and tasting room, visitors from all over the world have enjoyed sampling Heitz wines since 1961.
Photograph by Taryn Nycek

LEFT: Heitz Wine Cellars' cabernet sauvignons are allowed to age at an exceptionally slow pace, which includes two and a half years in French oak barrels.
Photograph by Robert Holmes

FACING PAGE LEFT: *Photograph courtesy of Heitz Wine Cellars*
FACING PAGE RIGHT: *Photograph by Robert M. Bruno*

NAPA VALLEY CHARDONNAY

GOURMET PAIRINGS

Irresistible to the eye as well as the palate, a seafood mélange of shrimp, mussels, and fresh fish resting lightly atop garden fresh vegetables harmonizes with the wine.

TASTING NOTES

Luminous and refreshing, the chardonnay is a classic. It is delightfully dry with a bracing varietal aroma and crisp citrus flavors that are subtle yet enticing, with a pleasing zest of lemon mid-palate. Well balanced with vivacious acidity and only the slightest hint of oak, the wine allows the fruit to shine as it builds to a clean, graceful finish.

WINEMAKER'S INSIGHT

The chardonnay is produced by combining fruit from several regions within the Napa Valley to achieve intriguing layers of flavor that are both crisp and rich.

TECHNICAL DATA

APPELLATION: Napa Valley
COMPOSITION: 100% chardonnay
MATURATION: Slightly oaked
CELLARING: A joy to drink today; will delight for the next several years
WEBSITE: www.heitzcellar.com

LEARN MORE

Learn more about Heitz Wine Cellars.

Hill Family Estate YOUNTVILLE

Drawn to Napa Valley by its beauty and emerging reputation as a world-class wine region, Doug Hill left his family farm and orchards near Healdsburg to work as a vineyard manager for the Jaeger family in Napa's fog-blanketed terrain. By the time he arrived in the valley, Napa was home to many established and renowned vineyards. However, Doug set out to explore the fringes of the valley's grape growing regions, eager to understand what could be grown in the outlaying hillsides and curious to experience the quality and character of the wine that could be produced.

ABOVE: Fog-blanketed hills near Yountville.
Photograph by Hilary Brodey

FACING PAGE: Sunset at Briarstone Vineyard in the Atlas Peak appellation.
Photograph by Jess Knubis

Doug wanted to raise his children with a shared appreciation for family and farming. The Hill family settled on an acre of land on the outskirts of Yountville, and children Ryan and Carly grew up playing in the vineyards and helping the neighbors grow organic produce for local restaurants, including Thomas Keller's world-renowned French Laundry.

TOP: Orchard at the farm in Yountville.

LEFT: Flowers at the farm in Yountville.

RIGHT: Doug and Ryan Hill in the vineyard.
Photographs by M. J. Wickham

FACING PAGE LEFT: *Photograph © iStockphoto.com/FocalHelicopter*
FACING PAGE RIGHT: *Photograph by M. J. Wickham*

TIARA SAUVIGNON BLANC

GOURMET PAIRINGS
Pair with oysters, clams, or flaky white fish, leafy green salad with vinaigrette, or roasted bell peppers.

TASTING NOTES
Rich melon and white peach aromas lead to a dimensional mouth-covering palate, ending with a clean, rich finish. Subtle notes of honeysuckle and tangerine tantalize the senses. It is a big wine and can be served with anything that lends itself to exotic tastes.

WINEMAKER'S INSIGHT
The Hill Family Estate Tiara is a sauvignon blanc made from a blend of vineyards, with a portion of sémillon. Tiara is created to make a rich, ripe, and creamy style of sauvignon blanc. We chose three clones and carefully selected the rootstalks so that the sauvignon blanc would have layers of complexity and interest.

TECHNICAL DATA

APPELLATION: Atlas Peak, Wooden Valley, American Canyon, and Oakville
COMPOSITION: Sauvignon blanc and sémillon
MATURATION: Six months in new French oak and cold fermentation tanks
CELLARING: Wonderful on release; drink within two to five years
WEBSITE: www.hillfamilyestate.com

WATCH A VIDEO

Vintner Doug Hill explains the history of Windy Flats and how its soil helps to create the beautiful character of Tiara Sauvignon Blanc.

STEWART RANCH PINOT NOIR

GOURMET PAIRINGS
Pair with pork or lamb, quinoa bean salad, or creamy Brie cheese. The wine is also excellent with pesto pasta dishes and fatty seafood like salmon.

TASTING NOTES
The wine boasts an inviting aroma of earthy milk chocolate with cloves and roses. The palate has intriguing surprises throughout, from a beautifully balanced raspberry and cherry soufflé texture—both light and dense—to cherries, roses, and dark spice that lead to a soft, melting finish.

WINEMAKER'S INSIGHT
Pinot noir grapes are high strung and their character does change with the year. The wine has that true pinot noir nose of red cherry, dark roses, and slightly earthy clove-spice. The palate is velvety and almost sweet with its red licorice fruit and "five spice" flavors. It grows over time after the cork is pulled, so I would expect it to deepen and expand with age.

TECHNICAL DATA

APPELLATION: Carneros
COMPOSITION: 100% pinot noir
MATURATION: 40% in new French oak, 60% in neutral French oak
CELLARING: Exquisite upon release; drink within five to seven years
WEBSITE: www.hillfamilyestate.com

LEARN MORE

Learn more about Hill Family Estate.

In the mid-1980s, the family began to plant their own vineyards, starting first with pinot noir in the Los Carneros appellation. Plantings of chardonnay, merlot, cabernet sauvignon, cabernet franc, sauvignon blanc, and albarino followed in a multitude of sites in the Oak Knoll, Atlas Peak, and Yountville appellations. The sites they chose to plant grapes in offer a range of different soils, climates, and growing conditions that create wines of unique character. Utilizing Doug's childhood passion for farming in a sustainable and environmentally friendly manner, Hill Family Estate continues to explore the ever-changing opportunities to create excellence in the vineyard.

ABOVE: Exterior of the Hill Family Estate tasting room in Yountville.
LEFT: Interior of the Hill Family Estate tasting room.
Photographs by M. J. Wickham

FACING PAGE LEFT: *Photograph by M. J. Wickham*
FACING PAGE RIGHT: *Photograph © iStockphoto.com/LauriPatterson*

Inglenook   RUTHERFORD

Founded in 1879, Inglenook began its life in Napa Valley with founder Gustave Niebaum, a world-traveled Finnish sea captain, at the helm. After Niebaum's passing, his grand-nephew John Daniel Jr. assumed control of the estate, continuing to craft exquisite wines under the mantra, "pride, not profit." After Daniel died, the winery was subdivided and sold to a series of wine conglomerates. In 1975, the Niebaum mansion captured the heart of one of Hollywood's greatest. Francis Ford Coppola, on a quest to find a summer home where he could get away from it all, discovered the mansion and its surrounding vineyards, and then began a 30-year quest to reunite the estate and restore its legacy.

ABOVE: Inglenook cabernet vineyards, a perfect expression of Rutherford dust.
FACING PAGE: Nestled in Rutherford, in the heart of Napa Valley, sits the majestic Inglenook château.
Photographs by M. J. Wickham

Despite the winery's size, Coppola immediately fell in love with the land and the founder's story, naming the winery Niebaum-Coppola Estate Winery in the French tradition. Twenty years later, the original vineyards were purchased, and the estate's château was restored to its former glory. In 2011, Francis and wife Eleanor purchased the trademark to Inglenook to restore the winery's original name. Today the winery features several intimate venues in which to enjoy seated tastings or private experiences: the bistro—where guests enjoy wines by the glass indoors or alfresco—a boutique stocked with merchandise personally selected by the Coppolas, and the winery museum, which pays homage to Inglenook and Hollywood.

TOP: Exquisite private events are hosted in the historic south barrel room.

ABOVE: Francis and Eleanor Coppola travel the world to hand-select rare and unique gifts for the Inglenook boutique.

LEFT: Guests of Inglenook can enjoy seated tastings of four estate wines. *Photographs by M. J. Wickham*

FACING PAGE: *Photographs by M. J. Wickham*

RUBICON

GOURMET PAIRINGS

Pair with pan-roasted squab with foie gras torchon, crispy prosciutto, summer truffles, and English peas. The combination of fatty, salty, and earthy flavors showcases the wine without overpowering the palate.

TASTING NOTES

Elegantly textured and rich in flavor, Rubicon delivers pronounced black cherry and cassis impressions with aromas of blueberries, dark chocolate, licorice, and spice. The wine possesses a fresh, ripe fruit entry and full-bodied palate with velvety tannins that linger into the finish.

WINEMAKER'S INSIGHT

With a focus on creating an elegant style of wine, the fruit was hand-selected at harvest, followed by an array of fermentation techniques to bring out the fruit. The wine was then barrel-aged in cool, temperature-controlled caves. Our Bordeaux winemaker Stephane Derenoncourt describes Rubicon as round and rich in the mouth with creaminess on the palate.

TECHNICAL DATA

APPELLATION: Rutherford
COMPOSITION: 87% cabernet sauvignon, 6% cabernet franc, 4% petit verdot, 3% merlot
MATURATION: 18 months in new and one-year-old small French oak barrels
CELLARING: Delightful upon release and for years to come
WEBSITE: www.inglenook.com

WATCH A VIDEO

Winemaker Philippe Bascaules discusses the complexity of Rubicon and all of Inglenook's wines.

Joseph Phelps Vineyards ST. HELENA

Joseph Phelps, a thriving Colorado builder, had his fate rerouted to Napa in the 1960s when he won the bid to build Souverain Winery, now Rutherford Hill Winery. He fell in love with the area, and by 1973 had purchased 600 acres of his own in Spring Valley, just outside of St. Helena, and crushed his first grapes. Joe's goal from the start was to craft Bordeaux, Rhône, and Burgundian varietals, and he was careful to pay close attention to soil and terroir when determining where to plant. The 1974 harvest brought the first vintages of Insignia—California's first proprietary blend of red Bordeaux varietals—and the nation's first wine labeled syrah. Such a frenzy of activity attracted attention, and Joseph Phelps Vineyards has held that notice and recognition ever since.

ABOVE: The Oval Room showcases original winery barrels for visiting guests.
FACING PAGE: The vineyards at Joseph Phelps Vineyards.
Photographs by M. J. Wickham

INSIGNIA

GOURMET PAIRINGS
Insignia pairs well with a grilled steak accompanied by a potato and fresh vegetable medley and an Insignia reduction sauce.

TASTING NOTES
Insignia boasts aromatic layers of blueberries, blackberries, and dark plums intertwined with roasted coffee, baking spices, currants, cigar box, and graphite. The seductive, velvety mouthfeel is lush with excellent length, intensely ripe black fruit, spice, and minerality that tie together seamlessly on the palate with incredible depth and concentration.

WINEMAKER'S INSIGHT
Only the best wine lots from our estate vineyards are selected for the Insignia blend. After hand-picking and sorting, grapes receive five days of cold soaking in stainless steel tanks before fermentation, followed by extended maceration of up to 40 days, adding the rich, vibrant hue, a fuller mouthfeel, and more concentrated, intense flavors prior to their aging for 24 months in 100-percent new French oak.

TECHNICAL DATA

APPELLATION: Napa Valley
COMPOSITION: Cabernet sauvignon; other red Bordeaux varietals
MATURATION: 24 months in 100% new French oak
CELLARING: Delicious upon release, though Insignia ages for decades
WEBSITE: www.josephphelps.com

WATCH A VIDEO

President Bill Phelps notes the advantages that Joseph Phelps Vineyards' flagship wine Insignia possesses, considering it has six estate vineyards to draw on.

Today Joe's son Bill acts as president, while vice-president and director of winemaking Damian Parker and winemaker Ashley Hepworth ensure the premium quality of the flagship wine, Insignia. The estate-grown portfolio also includes cabernet sauvignon, sauvignon blanc, syrah, viognier, Backus—a single-vineyard Oakville cabernet—and Eisrébe, a dessert wine made of scheurebe grapes. Every staff member embraces the dedication to great wine, attention to detail, and passion for winemaking that Joe himself championed. Joseph Phelps Vineyards consistently produces wines recognized as benchmarks and record-setters, not just throughout Napa Valley, but on the national and world stages as well.

TOP: President Bill Phelps oversees Joseph Phelps Vineyards.

ABOVE: The terrace is perfect for tasting and relaxing.

LEFT: The great hall plays host to a number of seminars conducted at the winery on a daily basis.
Photographs by M. J. Wickham

FACING PAGE: *Photographs by M. J. Wickham*

Keenan Winery ST. HELENA

The Keenan Winery estate sits on land first planted with vines in the late 19th century; such history may be the reason why Keenan wines have earned an across-the-board reputation for excellence, no matter the varietal. In 1974, Robert Keenan, driven by a love of the Spring Mountain region, sought a Mayacamas Range site to create a vineyard and winery. He found a place where 100 acres of zinfandel and syrah grew as the Conradi Winery until Prohibition forced it to close; by the time Robert purchased 180 acres of forest on the site, no vines were left. But as a mountaintop vineyard, the location was perfect. By the harvest of 1977, a newly reconstructed winery and 50 reclaimed acres of vineyards were in place.

ABOVE: The Upper Bowl vineyard is planted with cabernet franc, cabernet sauvignon, and merlot vines.

FACING PAGE: The arching cellar doorway, built in 1904, bears the chiseled initials P.C. at its top, paying homage to Peter Conradi and his family, who were the original settlers of the hillside property.
Photographs by M. J. Wickham

SPRING MOUNTAIN DISTRICT CHARDONNAY

GOURMET PAIRINGS
The food-worthy wine has a crisp acidity and medium body. One ideal pairing is grilled salmon with a sweet chili and soy vinaigrette with radicchio, endive, arugula lettuces, and fresh toy box tomatoes and avocado.

TASTING NOTES
The wine shows citrus, ripe pear, and green apple in the nose, with hints of lush white peach as it opens up. The sur lie aging has added richness and complexity, and plenty of oak character returns on the finish.

WINEMAKER'S INSIGHT
Our chardonnay clusters are hand-harvested, de-stemmed, and then gently pressed. The juice is fermented and aged in French and American oak barrels and the wine is left on the lees and the barrels stirred weekly. No secondary or malolactic fermentation is carried out, leading to the crisp, citrus character of the wine. Unlike most California chardonnays, it ages well.

TECHNICAL DATA

APPELLATION: Spring Mountain District
COMPOSITION: 100% chardonnay
MATURATION: Aged seven months in French and American oak barrels
CELLARING: Delicious now, or allow to age and develop rich caramelized characters
WEBSITE: www.keenanwinery.com

WATCH A VIDEO

President Michael Keenan talks about how the distinctive Spring Mountain District terroir enhances Keenan Winery wines.

Cabernet sauvignon, cabernet franc, chardonnay, merlot, and zinfandel grapes cover hillside areas, resulting in wines of exquisite complexity and intense flavor. Chardonnay, cabernet, and merlot wines in particular acquired notable success and popularity in the 1970s and '80s as full-bodied, well-balanced entries into the burgeoning Napa wine scene. Today the focus remains on those same three varietals—along with zinfandel, syrah, and "mernet," a merlot-cabernet blend—as the rich soil of the topography, sustainable farming practices, and an entirely solar-powered winery allow elegant estate wines to emerge naturally.

ABOVE: A picturesque picnic for six with a view of the chardonnay vineyard and Howell Mountain.

RIGHT: Some of the most beautiful and peaceful walks through the vineyards are in the rain.
Photographs by M. J. Wickham

FACING PAGE: *Photographs by M. J. Wickham*

Keenan Winery also encompasses a family legacy. Continuing the heritage, founder Robert's son Michael acts as winery president while his wife Jennifer designs the labels and consults on special event décor. Michael grew up on the property, so he's familiar with the high standards of quality set by his father. The Keenans and consulting winemaker Nils Venge ensure that wines improve in quality every year. Indeed, the team feels they've hit their stride and each vintage has been better than the one before—and considering the numerous accolades the winery has already gathered over the decades, that's no mean feat.

ABOVE LEFT: President Michael Keenan and wife Jennifer.

TOP: Keenan enthusiasts may relax and enjoy the wines with bread and cheeses while unwinding from the drive up Spring Mountain.

ABOVE: Steel and oak-steel fermentation tanks tower over stained oak barrels in the Keenan wine cellar.

FACING PAGE: The winery and vineyard are solar powered and sustainably farmed. Clone 4 chardonnay vines grow alongside pole-top mounted solar panels located at the end of every other vine row.
Photographs by M. J. Wickham

Kenzo Estate NAPA

Kenzo Tsujimoto is the epitome of originality and innovation; those who played "Space Invaders" in the 1970s are now sipping the exquisite wine he produces at Kenzo Estate. A pioneer in the gaming industry, Kenzo founded CapCom Co., Ltd. in 1983, a company which became one of the foremost game developers and publishers in the world. The company expanded to the United States in 1985, bringing it and Kenzo to Silicon Valley. Traveling between Japan and California, Kenzo developed an affinity for Napa Valley wines. In 1990, he purchased Kenzo Estate—formerly an Olympic equestrian facility known as Wild Horse Valley Ranch and located

ABOVE: Kenzo Estate corks decoratively fill glasses to add simple Wine Country elegance to the scenery.

FACING PAGE: The vineyard rows and rolling hills near one of the oldest residences of the estate.
Photographs by M. J. Wickham

RINDO RED WINE

GOURMET PAIRINGS

A beautiful Bordeaux blend, Rindo shows versatility for a cabernet. A delicate and savory shabu-shabu is the perfect accompaniment for the wine; perfect for anything from salmon to a dry-aged ribeye, hot off the grill.

TASTING NOTES

With ripe plum, blackberry jam, sandalwood, and black tea notes, the wine possesses aromas that are precise and delineated. With a bouquet of ripe red and black fruits, and backed with savory notes of bittersweet chocolate, coffee, and tobacco spice, the wine is lifted with a refreshing acidity before the plush texture of its velvety tannins finish in a lasting way.

WINEMAKER'S INSIGHT

Rindo, named for the purple gentian flower, is our flagship wine. The embodiment of the character of dozens of vineyard blocks on the estate, Rindo is composed of an array of varietal components fermented separately in small tanks before being held in French oak for 20 months. Together the varietals create a harmonious wine.

TECHNICAL DATA

APPELLATION: Napa Valley
COMPOSITION: 37.3% cabernet sauvignon, 28.8% merlot, 27.5% cabernet franc, 4.9% petit verdot, 1.6% malbec
MATURATION: 20 months in 60% new French oak
CELLARING: Delicious upon release, but will age beautifully for 10 to 15 years
WEBSITE: www.kenzoestate.com

LEARN MORE

Learn more about Kenzo Estate.

TOP: The upper terrace and the tasting room.

ABOVE: The Kenzo Estate logo adorns a gate when entering the vineyards.

ABOVE RIGHT: One of the many lakes on the property is inhabited by natural wildlife, including smallmouth bass.
Photographs by M. J. Wickham

FACING PAGE: Photographs courtesy of Kenzo Estate

in the Wild Horse Valley appellation—to pursue his newfound passion.

Under the direction of consulting winemaker Heidi Peterson Barrett, Kenzo Estate produces an array of varietals: sauvignon blanc, cabernet sauvignon, merlot, cabernet franc, petit verdot, and malbec. Heidi began her career under the direction of Napa winemakers and became one herself in 1983, at the age of 25, at Buehler Vineyards. She quickly gained notoriety for her unique winemaking style, so much so that Robert Parker Jr. called her "The First Lady of Wine" and *TIME* magazine dubbed her "The Wine Diva of Napa Valley."

Together Heidi and Kenzo Estate craft elegant and well-balanced wines with personality.

Kenzo's passions for wine and conservation are obvious: only three percent of the estate is developed for the vineyard and winery. The rest remains a natural landscape and a testament to his desire to preserve the scenery of Napa Valley. Just as Kenzo travels to and from Japan, Kenzo Estate wines may be enjoyed in the estate's tasting rooms in both Tokyo and Osaka, transporting the spirit of Napa Valley across the globe.

ABOVE LEFT: The entrance to the tasting room lit up in the evening.

TOP: Barrels are lined up single-stack within the expansive caves.

ABOVE: Concreted fermenters imported from Burgundy line one of the walls in the production area.
Photographs by M. J. Wickham

FACING PAGE: *Photographs courtesy of Kenzo Estate*

ASATSUYU SAUVIGNON BLANC

GOURMET PAIRINGS

Fresh sushi and the cleanest uses of miso showcase the wine. Summer salads with tomatoes, avocado, and crab highlight the wine's delicate nuances. For something heartier, try creamy risotto with Dungeness crab.

TASTING NOTES

The wine is crisp and focused with layers of stone fruit interlaced with orange peel and lychee. The flavors mingle with a fresh, distinctly sauvignon blanc acidity with floral hints of gooseberry, lime zest, grapefruit, lemongrass, and kiwi.

WINEMAKER'S INSIGHT

As Heidi Barrett's only sauvignon blanc, Asatsuyu is unique among whites. Translated as "morning dew," Asatsuyu retains the terroir of the appellation through its small barrel aging and suppression of malolactic fermentation.

TECHNICAL DATA

APPELLATION: Napa Valley
COMPOSITION: 100% sauvignon blanc
MATURATION: Seven months in 50% neutral French oak and 50% stainless steel barrels
CELLARING: Cellar Asatsuyu for at least two years to develop its full weight on the palate
WEBSITE: www.kenzoestate.com

LEARN MORE

Learn more about Kenzo Estate.

Morlet Family Vineyards & Winery ST. HELENA

Morlet Family Vineyards & Winery brings French winemaking techniques to Napa through its winemaker, Luc Morlet, who grew up as part of his family's fourth generation of winemakers in France. Luc and wife Jodie founded the label in 2006 and today run the winery from a historic St. Helena estate restored to its original 1880 beauty. Morlet wines embody a relentless search for the utmost in quality. Luc's pedigree is impeccable: He learned vineyard farming and winemaking firsthand on his parents' Avenay-Val-d'Or domaine in the Champagne region of France, and earned degrees in viticulture, enology, and wine business. During graduate school, he interned at prestigious wineries throughout Burgundy, Bordeaux,

ABOVE: The Morlet family's vineyards include the Mon Chevalier cabernet sauvignon vineyard located in Knights Valley and overlooking majestic Mount St. Helena.
Photograph courtesy of Morlet Family Vineyards & Winery

FACING PAGE: Jodie and Luc Morlet live by their winery's motto, "manicured vineyards, classical winemaking, and creative artisanship," which results in highly sought-after and strictly allocated wines.
Photograph by M. J. Wickham

Champagne, and the southwest of France and toured many European wine regions. Luc's early career included making the wines at Chanson Père et Fils in Burgundy, before moving to St. Helena in 1993 to replace the winemaker of a French subsidiary. After a few years back in France perfecting his Bordeaux crafting at Château Dauzac in Margaux, he returned to Napa in 1996 to marry his California sweetheart, Jodie, and make the wines at Newton Vineyard. For many years following, Luc enjoyed a role as one of Napa's most sought-after winemakers, thanks to his dizzying array of heritage, education, and expertise.

ABOVE: Luc and Jodie Morlet restored the historic pre-Prohibition winery, originally built by William Castner in 1880.

LEFT: Paul, Luc, Jodie, and Claire Morlet along with their dog, Chocolate, stand near the 1853 Victorian farmhouse located on their estate. *Photographs by M. J. Wickham*

FACING PAGE: *Photographs by M. J. Wickham; dish courtesy of Hiro Sone and Lissa Doumani, Terra Restaurant*

MORLET ESTATE

GOURMET PAIRINGS
The elegance of Morlet Estate carries well through each bite of Liberty Farm duck breast served alongside a chestnut yam purée. Its silky tannins highlight the sweetness of the roasted baby turnips and the drizzled huckleberry sauce.

TASTING NOTES
The wine's dark and deep hue of bright ruby red complements an intense and complex bouquet of red cherry and blackberry intermixed with notes of minerals—graphite, wet river rocks—and licorice, fresh blond tobacco, and a hint of fresh blackcurrant. Full bodied, the harmonious palate is reminiscent of the nose, with a round frame and an outstanding finesse, building up to a long, seamless, and elegant finish.

WINEMAKER'S INSIGHT
This collectible wine comes exclusively from the charming estate that Jodie and Luc purchased in 2010. Located in the beautiful St. Helena appellation, just north of the town, the vineyard is planted in 100-percent cabernet sauvignon vines and benefits from a sunny mountain climate and well-draining alluvial and volcanic soils. Handcrafted with classical winemaking techniques, this wine shows tremendous finesse and elegance and is built to age for decades.

TECHNICAL DATA

APPELLATION: St. Helena
COMPOSITION: 100% cabernet sauvignon
MATURATION: 10 years
CELLARING: 25 years and up
WEBSITE: www.morletwines.com

WATCH A VIDEO

Jodie and Luc Morlet explain the history of the winery and the winemaking philosophy behind Morlet Estate.

PASSIONNÉMENT

GOURMET PAIRINGS
Its opulence marries beautifully with the melting texture of Brandt New York striploin, served with caramelized cipollini onions and roasted baby carrots; complements thick reduction and rich foie gras sauces.

TASTING NOTES
The wine's color is dark purple, with an intense and complex bouquet of berries intermixed with notes of crème de cassis, plum, and a hint of cedar and cigar box. Full bodied, the palate has a creamy texture and a great intensity reminiscent of the nose. Luscious tannins, intense aromatic complexity, and opulence create a flamboyant yet harmonious ensemble, leading to a very long, complex, and smooth finish.

WINEMAKER'S INSIGHT
Featuring the close interaction of a beautiful Oakville bench vineyard and Luc and Jodie's manicured vineyard on the foothills of Knights Valley, a passionate, uncompromised, and ongoing pursuit of quality characterizes the wine. As the French say, "*Je t'aime, un peu, beaucoup, passionnément!*" meaning: "I love you, a little, a lot, passionately!" The judicious blend draws on only the finest barrels. Luc dedicates this special wine to his wife, Jodie.

TECHNICAL DATA

APPELLATION: Oakville
COMPOSITION: 100% cabernet sauvignon
MATURATION: 10 years
CELLARING: 25 years and up
WEBSITE: www.morletwines.com

WATCH A VIDEO

Founders Luc and Jodie discuss the craft and inspiration behind Passionnément.

By 2006, after creating and contributing to several famed vintages for the highly sought-after Peter Michael Winery, Luc was ready to produce wine under his own label. He describes his winemaking philosophy as "neo-classic laissez-faire without compromise," pursuing the highest quality and letting that speak for itself. The label sources fruit from unique Napa Valley and Sonoma County vineyards, including two owned by Luc and Jodie. The finest French oak, best bottling supplies, carefully selected Sardinia corks, locally made foils and labels—everything about Morlet speaks to premium standards. The unique portfolio includes chardonnay, pinot noir, cabernet sauvignon, syrah, and original blends. The Morlet style results in wines which are harmonious in their intensity, richness, complexity, and refinement.

ABOVE LEFT: The Morlet wines age in French oak barrels imported by Luc and Jodie from two of the finest artisan coopers: Vincent Darnajou of Bordeaux and Gauthier Frères of Burgundy.
Photograph by M. J. Wickham

TOP: In an ongoing pursuit of quality, Luc designed the Le Trieur sorting machine, which facilitates berry-per-berry sorting.
Photograph by Curt Fischer Photographs

ABOVE: Luc and Jodie's commitment to handcrafting harmonious wines inspired their label logo, based upon 19th-century French artist Mathurin Moreau's sculpture, *L'Harmonie*.
Photograph by M. J. Wickham

FACING PAGE: *Photographs by M. J. Wickham; dish courtesy of Hiro Sone and Lissa Doumani, Terra Restaurant*

Mumm Napa RUTHERFORD

Totally pure in its sense of pedigree and place, Mumm Napa brings together the very best of the renowned Napa Valley and celebrated Champagne, France. As uncompromising in quality as it is unpretentious in character, Mumm Napa crafts world-class sparkling wines that offer a luxurious sense of indulgence. The story of this popular destination and equally popular sparkling wine began in 1979, when the legendary French champagne house of G. H. Mumm began its quest to find the ideal grape growing area in the United States in a top-secret venture, "Project Lafayette," headed by Guy Devaux. Growing up in Champagne, France, Devaux was the ideal choice given his more than 40 years' experience crafting still wines,

ABOVE: Mumm Napa is located on the Silverado Trail in Rutherford.
Photograph courtesy of Mumm Napa

FACING PAGE: The Devaux Vineyard in the Carneros appellation of Napa Valley.
Photograph by M. J. Wickham

sparkling wines, and luxury champagnes, spanning across four continents.

Devaux quietly searched the Wine Country, surreptitiously buying grapes and small lots of wine he considered outstanding. His only rule was to find a terroir where he could create wine from the traditional champagne grape varieties while using only the highest quality méthode traditionnelle winemaking process that originated in Champagne over a century ago. Ultimately Devaux found his prize in Napa Valley, and Mumm Napa was born.

Today Champagne-born winemaker Ludovic Dervin carries forward the legacy, marrying the exacting fruit and innovation of the Napa Valley along with the traditional champagne-making methods to craft bright and finely distinctive sparkling wines. Mumm Napa is also noted for its commitment to fine art photography, featuring two galleries. One showcases 28 original prints by the legendary photographer Ansel Adams, while the second gallery has rotating exhibits featuring

ABOVE LEFT: Noted for its friendly staff, outstanding sparkling wines, and spectacular vineyard views, Mumm Napa invites visitors to its two tasting patios and indoor salon.
Photograph by M. J. Wickham

TOP: Guided tours—which feature a tasting of three different sparkling wines—present guests with the process of producing champagne method sparkling wine.
Photograph by M. J. Wickham

ABOVE: While seated under the 180-year-old oak tree on the Oak Terrace overlooking the vineyards, guests enjoy exclusive tastings of library wines and cheese pairings.
Photograph courtesy of Mumm Napa

FACING PAGE LEFT: *Photograph by M. J. Wickham*
FACING PAGE RIGHT: *Photograph courtesy of Mumm Napa*

BLANC DE BLANCS

GOURMET PAIRINGS
Pair with watermelon, Wild Boar Farms heirloom tomatoes, and tri-color roasted baby beet salad with verjus vinaigrette.

TASTING NOTES
The nose offers a bracing blend of fresh golden apples, ripe pear, and lemon with a hint of melon and white blossoms. The pinot gris influence gifts the wine with a full, fleshy body and is a spicy accent to the chardonnay's deep structure and crisp flavor. Nuances of warm brioche, crème brûlée, toasted nuts, and vanilla beans come through thanks to the maturation process.

WINEMAKER'S INSIGHTS
The Blanc de Blancs is a refreshing blend of chardonnay and pinot gris. The chardonnay provides a crisp acidity and citrus notes, while the pinot gris complements with fuller stone fruit tones and spice components.

TECHNICAL DATA

APPELLATION: Napa Valley
COMPOSITION: 90% chardonnay, 10% pinot gris
MATURATION: 36 months of fermentation; yeast-aged three years in the bottle
CELLARING: Exquisite upon release; may be enjoyed for years to come
WEBSITE: www.mummnapa.com

WATCH A VIDEO

Ludovic Dervin, winemaker at Mumm Napa, discusses how climate nuances enhance the character of the winery's Blanc de Blancs.

DVX ROSÉ

GOURMET PAIRINGS
Pair with grilled sockeye salmon with grilled asparagus and pear tomato, and cured lemon salad with fig vincotto and Napa Valley extra virgin olive oil.

TASTING NOTES
This exquisite wine shows with a soft salmon glow, pleasant aromas of fresh plum, strawberry, and spice. The texture is delicate and silky with notes of currant, clove, and fresh-baked biscuits that linger on the palate.

WINEMAKER'S INSIGHT
Only a few premium lots of chardonnay and pinot noir are selected for the DVX Rosé blend. Part of the wine was barrel fermented to add depth and spiciness. The blend was yeast-aged an average of four years in bottles and disgorged as a brut style. The DVX Rosé is the most delicate and elegant wine in the portfolio and is sure to make every occasion special.

TECHNICAL DATA

APPELLATION: Napa Valley
COMPOSITION: 53% pinot noir, 47% chardonnay
MATURATION: Yeast-aged an average of four years in the bottle
CELLARING: Elegant upon release; wonderful for years to come
WEBSITE: www.mummnapa.com

WATCH A VIDEO

Winemaker Ludovic Dervin explains the characteristics of Mumm Napa's DVX Rosé.

renowned fine art photographers from around the world.

One of the primary sources of high-quality fruit comes from Mumm Napa's Devaux Vineyard, situated in the cool southern Carneros region of Napa Valley. The vineyard possesses some of the finest, most ancient soils, including the first limestone outcropping found in the area. Limestone, a major component of the soil in France's Champagne region, creates depth and richness in the fruit.

ABOVE: The fine art photography galleries feature a private collection of iconic Ansel Adams prints, the works of established masters, and art by new photographers.

RIGHT: Guests enjoy a complimentary tour as the winery opens its doors for the day. Visitors are educated on the intricate process of producing sparkling wine.
Photographs by M. J. Wickham

FACING PAGE LEFT: *Photograph courtesy of Mumm Napa*
FACING PAGE RIGHT: *Photograph by M. J. Wickham*

O'Connell Family Vineyard   YOUNTVILLE

Gabrielle and Wayne O'Connell have winemaking in their blood. Gabrielle hails from a family of wine and culinary experts, well traveled gourmands, and wine aficionados. Wayne grew up in an Italian household and gained his early education and wine experience at his grandfather's side, making wine in the family cellar. Thanks to their early exposure to the winemaking world, both had long-time dreams of owning a winery. The couple purchased vineyard acreage in Yountville and founded O'Connell Family Vineyard in 2000.

ABOVE: Inspired by the Impressionist painter Monet, apricot, blue, and pale yellow flowers create the perfect spot to sip an afternoon glass of sauvignon blanc.
Photograph by M. J. Wickham

FACING PAGE: Ancient valley oaks grace sweeping lawns of the historic estate. A mosaic of "garden rooms"—the Japanese Woodland, Rhododendron, and Rose Gardens—enhance lush grounds.
Photograph courtesy of O'Connell Family Vineyard

The O'Connells believe in a very hands-on process of winemaking; they understand that not every part of the vineyard ripens at exactly the same time, so each block harvest is based on individual optimal ripening. Gabrielle personally selects the specific rows of fruit for each harvest, and each varietal—cabernet sauvignon, petit verdot, and carménère—is vinted separately. Rather than base the bottling of the wine on aging in the barrel, the techniques instead revolve around the taste of the wine and not a specific timeframe.

ABOVE: All generations are involved in the wine industry, are inspired by the healthy lifestyle of being on the land, and share an appreciation of its bounty.
Photograph by M. J. Wickham

LEFT: Guests are welcome to sip the estate wines while relaxing by the pond and fountain.
Photograph courtesy of O'Connell Family Vineyard

FACING PAGE: *Photographs by M. J. Wickham*

ESTATE GROWN CABERNET SAUVIGNON

GOURMET PAIRINGS

Pair with rich meats like steak or lamb or fatty fish like salmon.

TASTING NOTES

A dense wine that satisfies the senses, it boasts provocative aromas of dark fruit, laced with exotic spices. Flavors of red fruits, cedar, cardamom, nutmeg, tobacco, and dark chocolate dance on the palate when drinking this elegant and richly textured wine.

WINEMAKER'S INSIGHT

The meticulously crafted wine blends the flavors of our distinctive blocks, which lay at the place of convergence of volcanic soils from the eastern mountains, the alluvial soils from the Mayacamas Mountains in the west, and sand and gravel from Dry Creek. The ideal climate of warm days and fog-cooled nights allows our grapes to ripen over a long growing season, resulting in a graceful wine.

TECHNICAL DATA

APPELLATION: Oak Knoll District Napa Valley
COMPOSITION: 98% cabernet sauvignon, 2% petit verdot
MATURATION: 42 months in French oak barrels
CELLARING: Enjoy upon release; cellars well for up to 10 years
WEBSITE: www.gabriellewine.com

WATCH A VIDEO

Vintner Gabrielle Leonhard discusses the unique soil structure that contributes to O'Connell Family Vineyard's terroir-specific wines.

SILVER STALLION CABERNET SAUVIGNON

GOURMET PAIRINGS
Pair with rich meats or dark chocolate.

TASTING NOTES
The power of cabernet sauvignon meets the earthiness of malbec. Available in magnums only to celebrate the six generations of Cattleman's history.

WINEMAKER'S INSIGHT
Our wines have a focus on the fifth sense: the umami factor, which translates into mouthfeel. This velvety textural quality gives additional pleasure to a sip of wine as it envelops the palate. Our winemaking practice of minimal intervention produces approachable wine with supple tannins and expressive fruit within an elegant and balanced structure.

TECHNICAL DATA

APPELLATION: Napa Valley
COMPOSITION: Cabernet sauvignon and malbec
MATURATION: 24 months in French oak
CELLARING: Elegant upon release and for years to come
WEBSITE: www.gabriellewine.com

WATCH A VIDEO

Gabrielle Leonhard, vintner at O'Connell Family Vineyard, tells the story of Silver Stallion.

A sense of community permeates O'Connell Family Vineyard, and part of that philosophy depends upon organic and sustainable farming of the vines. Gabrielle and Wayne have embraced biodiversity; the grapevines are surrounded by herb gardens, fruit trees, and mature eucalyptus trees. Organic lavender, olive trees, and historic apple trees grow on the estate. While these plantings yield marketable products themselves, the communal state of nature at the vineyard is primarily supportive of growing healthy grapes. The grapes provide delicious wine, which pairs with the herbed salts, lavender-infused honey, and extra virgin olive oil cultivated from the gardens, and the gardens in turn give health back to the vineyard soil. In much the same way, the entire winemaking team works together to create the estate's wines, many of which are set to be collector's items.

TOP: The original retreat of silent Hollywood movie actress Lenore Sterns.
Photograph by M. J. Wickham

ABOVE: Organically grown olives, lavender, fruit trees, vegetables, and herbs surround vineyard blocks to enhance biodiversity.
Photographs courtesy of O'Connell Family Vineyard

FACING PAGE: *Photographs by M. J. Wickham*

Peju Province Winery — RUTHERFORD

When Tony and Herta "H.B." Peju relocated to Rutherford from Los Angeles, they brought with them a vision to build a winery, an unwavering work ethic, and two young daughters who soaked in the couple's entrepreneurial spirit and love for Napa's beautiful farmland. The Rutherford ranch they purchased had been planted with grapes since the early 1900s. With a strong background in horticulture, Tony began farming and harvesting the property's grapes himself; it wasn't long before he realized the extraordinary potential of the vineyard and started making his own wine. The family has since acquired additional properties in Pope Valley and Calistoga, and adopted environmentally conscious farming practices.

The Rutherford Estate Vineyard is certified organic, while the Persephone

ABOVE: The winery's gardens and iconic sycamore trees at dusk.
FACING PAGE: Peju Province Winery in the heart of Rutherford.
Photographs courtesy of Peju Province Winery

and Tess vineyards in Pope Valley and the Wappo Vineyard in Calistoga are sustainably farmed. The winery's tasting room resides in a 50-foot tower built in 2003 that was envisioned by Tony Peju even before he purchased the property. Originally designed by architect Calvin Straub in 1981, the pen and ink rendering has graced the label of every Peju Province Winery wine.

Daughters Lisa and Ariana are fully engaged in their family's business. As the winery's sales ambassador, Lisa is always on the go—maintaining and establishing relationships with restaurant and distributor partners, and attending winemaker dinners and trade and consumer events. Ariana manages Peju's daily business operations. She is also responsible for a number of important environmental initiatives, including the "Harvesting the Sun" project, which installed 720 solar panels on the winery roof and provides 40 percent of Peju's energy.

The care put into the winery's French provincial building, its beautiful gardens, and the sustainable initiatives are expressions of Peju wines—excellence in operations that coincides with excellence in winemaking. The Peju family's philosophy centers around the fact that nature will follow its own course if allowed, but it is the sculpting of that nature that produces the finest wine possible from that natural setting.

TOP: The lovingly tended gardens are decorated with sculptures.

ABOVE: H.B., Ariana, Lisa, and Tony Peju.

RIGHT: Sustainably grown grapes on the Persephone Vineyard in Pope Valley.

FACING PAGE TOP: Beautiful stained glass at the winery.

FACING PAGE BOTTOM: The entrance to the winery's French provincial building.
Photographs courtesy of Peju Province Winery

THIS PAGE: *Photograph courtesy of Peju Province Winery*
FACING PAGE LEFT: *Photograph © iStockphoto.com/HannamariaH*
FACING PAGE RIGHT: *Photograph © iStockphoto.com/swalls*

CABERNET SAUVIGNON RESERVE

GOURMET PAIRINGS
Exceptional with slow-braised meats such as oxtail and shortribs or savory-sweet preparations like duck with wild huckleberry sauce, it may also be enjoyed with rich, earthy, stewed wild mushrooms.

TASTING NOTES
Peju's Cabernet Sauvignon Reserve is a classic Rutherford blend of voluptuous and sultry fruit with youthful exuberance. The aromas of black currant, cassis, and black raspberry lead to hints of white pepper, anise, cedar, and sage. Flavors of rich blackberry cobbler and black cherries are punctuated by holiday spice and cigar box. Beautiful, rich fruit tannins linger through a soft and supple finish.

WINEMAKER'S INSIGHT
At the heart of Napa Valley lies the famed Rutherford Bench, an alluvial fan consisting of low-yielding loam, sand, and gravel soil in which cabernet sauvignon thrives. Fruit for our Cabernet Sauvignon Reserve is 100-percent estate-grown and organically farmed on our Rutherford Vineyard, which yields a distinct expression of ripe blackberries and dusty spice.

TECHNICAL DATA

APPELLATION: Rutherford
COMPOSITION: 100% cabernet sauvignon
MATURATION: 26 months in 85% new French oak barrels
CELLARING: Enjoy upon release or for up to 10 years
WEBSITE: www.peju.com

H.B. CABERNET SAUVIGNON

GOURMET PAIRINGS
An elegant, refined Bordeaux-style blend, the H.B. calls for an indulgent pairing of tenderloin with black truffle demi-glace or a high-low splurge such as a burger made of Kobe beef with foie gras on a brioche bun.

TASTING NOTES
The H.B. Cabernet Sauvignon displays aromas of opulent black fruits, tobacco, and coffee with earthy undercurrents of leather and cedar. Beautifully focused flavors of plum and blackberry carry into cassis, bittersweet chocolate, and dried figs. This classic Rutherford wine offers pure fruit expression with rich, concentrated, complex character and luscious tannins that give way to a memorable and lengthy finish.

WINEMAKER'S INSIGHT
The fruit is hand-picked from the H.B. block of our organically farmed estate vineyard, then hand-sorted before an extended maceration and fermentation in small one-ton bins.

TECHNICAL DATA

APPELLATION: Rutherford
COMPOSITION: 91% cabernet sauvignon, 8% merlot, 1% petit verdot
MATURATION: 30 months in 80% new French oak barrels
CELLARING: Enjoy now or cellar for 15-plus years
WEBSITE: www.peju.com

LEARN MORE

Learn more about Peju Province Winery.

Robert Mondavi Winery OAKVILLE

At the age of 53, with little money but full of energy and vision, Robert Mondavi changed the course of the U.S. wine industry. Realizing a long-held dream to create excellent Napa Valley wines that would stand in the company of the great wines of the world, he founded the iconic Robert Mondavi Winery in 1966. For the home of his fledgling winery, he chose a site in the middle of the To Kalon Vineyard, a historic property long regarded for producing some of Napa Valley's finest cabernet sauvignons and sauvignon blancs.

A steady pursuit of innovation and excellence ruled from the beginning, and by the late 1960s the winery had introduced cold fermentation, stainless

ABOVE: *Welcome Muse* adorns the front lawn of the winery.

FACING PAGE: Beniamino Bufano's *Bear* sculpture greets visitors.
Photographs courtesy of Robert Mondavi Winery

steel tanks, and the use of small French oak barrels to the nascent California wine industry. He made history when he coined the term "fumé blanc" for a dry style of sauvignon blanc. Other innovations, such as gentle winemaking techniques that increase wine quality and natural farming practices that protect people and the environment, have led to fundamental changes in the industry's approach to grape growing.

The cultural and culinary arts programs at Robert Mondavi Winery are showplaces for painters, sculptors, photographers, jazz and classical musicians, and the great chefs of the world, begun when cultural activities at wineries were a radical idea. The winery led the way with events such as the annual summer music festival, art shows, and the Great Chefs program, established

in 1976 as the first winery culinary program in America.

With a firm conviction that the personality of great wine is a result of soil, climate, vineyard management, and winemaking philosophy, the winery continues to pursue Mondavi's goal of excellence with the same passion and innovative spirit. Robert Mondavi Winery has led California's wine industry—and much of the world—with innovations in grape growing and winemaking, as well as educational and cultural outreach.

ABOVE: Robert Mondavi Winery celebrates wine, cuisine, and the arts.
Photograph courtesy of Robert Mondavi Winery

RIGHT & FACING PAGE: Some of the region's oldest grapes grow from the To Kalon Vineyard.
Photographs © Erich Weiss

THIS PAGE: Photograph courtesy of Robert Mondavi Winery
FACING PAGE LEFT: Photograph © iStockphoto.com/kcline
FACING PAGE RIGHT: Photograph © iStockphoto.com/AngiePhotos

FUMÉ BLANC RESERVE

GOURMET PAIRINGS
The wine pairs well with grilled seafood or crab cakes.

TASTING NOTES
Delicate aromas of bright citrus and lush tropical and floral flavors lead to concentrated tones of mineral and herbal nuances. Bright and balanced acidity establishes the expressive flavor profile. Spices are revealed with a subtle foundation of creamy oak. An elegant texture and nice weight finish the wine.

WINEMAKER'S INSIGHT
The hand-harvested grapes are picked in the cool morning hours, carefully sorted in our To Kalon Cellar to remove any sunburned clusters, and are gently whole-cluster pressed to capture the vibrant fruit character. To enhance creaminess and integrated flavors, the wine is stirred and aged sur lie in French oak barrels.

TECHNICAL DATA
APPELLATION: Oakville District
COMPOSITION: 96% sauvignon blanc, 4% sémillon
MATURATION: Aged nine months in French oak barrels, sur lie
CELLARING: Delightful upon release; wonderful for years to come
WEBSITE: www.robertmondaviwinery.com

CABERNET SAUVIGNON RESERVE

GOURMET PAIRINGS
Exquisite with beef dishes with mushrooms or rich sauces.

TASTING NOTES
Dark cherry and blueberry aromas mingle with a hint of black olive and sage to create the cabernet's base. Notes of dark chocolate and coffee, along with its ripe tannins, provide an elegant finish.

WINEMAKER'S INSIGHT
Hand-harvested into small bins and hand-sorted on tables in our To Kalon Fermentation, the wine is cellared using gravity-flow movement of must and wine fermented in traditional oak tanks and gently pressed in a wooden basket press for 40 days of extended skin contact in oak tanks to soften and integrate the tannins.

TECHNICAL DATA
APPELLATION: Oakville District
COMPOSITION: 85% cabernet sauvignon, 8% cabernet franc, 7% petit verdot
MATURATION: Aged 18 months in 100% new French oak barrels
CELLARING: Enjoy upon release; cellar for six to 10 years
WEBSITE: www.robertmondaviwinery.com

LEARN MORE

Learn more about Robert Mondavi Winery.

Rombauer Vineyards   ST. HELENA

It wasn't Koerner and Joan Rombauer's intention to start a winery on the 40 acres the couple purchased in 1972, but a few years after moving to Napa Valley they heeded their passion for wine and jumped into the wine business, helping to found Conn Creek Winery in 1976. Shortly thereafter, they decided to concentrate on building their own family winery and soon released the first vintage of Rombauer Vineyards: the 1980 Cabernet Sauvignon. Rombauer's commitment to growing the highest quality fruit has been a directive from Koerner from the start, and each member of the

ABOVE: Zinfandel vines at Rombauer Vineyards.

FACING PAGE: The Napa Valley view from Rombauer Vineyards.
Photographs by M. J. Wickham

CARNEROS CHARDONNAY

GOURMET PAIRINGS
Pairs exceptionally well with grilled meats, seafood, light pasta, or salads.

TASTING NOTES
Golden yellow in color with a pale hue, the wine boasts seductive aromas of melon, citrus, and peach on the palate, backed with a lively acidity. Balanced with honeysuckle and vanilla, the wine has an added creamy dimension that finishes with a satisfying buttery complexity.

WINEMAKER'S INSIGHT
We have a unique style of chardonnay that has developed over time with grapes from select vineyards from the Carneros region. The cool climate and clay soils offer ideal conditions for chardonnay grapes.

TECHNICAL DATA

APPELLATION: Carneros
COMPOSITION: 100% chardonnay
MATURATION: 10 months in American and French oak barrels
CELLARING: Exquisite upon release, the wine also develops and evolves with bottle age
WEBSITE: www.rombauer.com

WATCH A VIDEO

Vintner K.R. Rombauer talks about the flavors and characteristics of Rombauer chardonnay.

family contributes to the winery's daily management and operations.

The family's love of food and wine becomes abundantly clear once a bottle of Rombauer Vineyards wine is uncorked. Right on the cork is the sentiment "The Joy of Wine" in honor of Koerner's great-aunt, Irma

TOP: Cave door at Rombauer Vineyards.

ABOVE: Sheana, K.R., Koerner, and Sandy Rombauer.

LEFT: "Cabernet Point" at the winery.
Photographs by M. J. Wickham

FACING PAGE: *Photographs by M. J. Wickham*

Rombauer, who wrote the classic *Joy of Cooking* cookbook in 1931. The dedication and passion Koerner and his family have for the wine business and Napa Valley continue to encourage winemaker Richie Allen to push for excellence with every vintage. While acknowledging that great wines start in the vineyard, Koerner and Richie are always working to improve what happens in the cellars to continue producing award-winning wines that include cabernet sauvignon, chardonnay, merlot, and zinfandel. The Rombauers welcome guests to their hilltop winery near St. Helena in hopes of sharing the same love of wine that has inspired them since the winery's founding.

ABOVE: Inside the caves at Rombauer Vineyards.

LEFT: Bacchus guards the caves.
Photographs by M. J. Wickham

FACING PAGE: *Photographs by M. J. Wickham*

CABERNET SAUVIGNON, NAPA VALLEY

GOURMET PAIRINGS
Serve with rich meats such as beef, duck, or lamb.

TASTING NOTES
Dark plum in color with a hue of crimson red, the wine boasts an opulent bouquet of blackberry, red currant, plum, and dark cherry fruit. The flavors intertwine with spice notes for an exceptionally balanced palate. Smooth tannins help build depth on the back palate for a rich, lengthy finish of creamy vanilla and blackberry.

WINEMAKER'S INSIGHT
The fruit for this cabernet come from our vineyards in Stags Leap, Atlas Peak, St. Helena, and Calistoga. To ensure optimum quality and fruit expression, we control every aspect, from farming each vineyard to bottling the wine.

TECHNICAL DATA

APPELLATION: Napa Valley
COMPOSITION: 88% cabernet sauvignon, 7% petit verdot, 5% cabernet franc
MATURATION: 19 months in French oak
CELLARING: Exquisite upon release, the wine also develops and evolves with bottle age and may be enjoyed for 10 years
WEBSITE: www.rombauer.com

WATCH A VIDEO

Vintner K. R. Rombauer presents the winery's Cabernet Sauvignon.

Round Pond Estate — RUTHERFORD

World-class vineyards, gardens, and orchards compose the 356-acre Round Pond Estate located in the heart of Rutherford, a veritable Napa Valley paradise characterized by an abiding love of the land. It's the realization of a dream envisioned by founder Bob MacDonnell, who spent childhood summers camping by a place called Round Pond near Lake Frederick in West Point, New York. In 1983, he set out to create a natural and serene family retreat focused on growing extraordinary grapes for the valley's best wineries. Today Round Pond Estate harnesses a combination of organic and sustainable techniques to farm exceptional fruit, which is then used to produce its own fine artisanal wines, olive oils, and vinegars.

ABOVE: The historic Red Pole Barn at Round Pond.

FACING PAGE: The entrance drive to Round Pond Estate—opened to guests in 2007—is framed by elegant California palms.
Photographs by M. J. Wickham

"Gourmet" encapsulates Round Pond, and the family and team maintain rigorous quality standards by controlling as much of the process as possible. Whether utilizing the state-of-the-art technology in the Round Pond winery and olive mill, carefully tending the grapevines and olive trees daily, hand-harvesting the fruit, or blending and bottling by hand, team members honor a commitment to excellence. The vineyard grows cabernet sauvignon in one of the most ideal locations for the grape around, and Italian and Spanish olives flourish on the land as well. Visitors to Round Pond Estate discover an array of delicious wines and gourmet products—as well as a breathtaking view of the valley—and come away awed by how skillfully the growers and winemakers cull the best the land has to offer and bottle it up.

ABOVE LEFT: An estate tasting of Round Pond's cabernet sauvignon and sauvignon blanc awaits guests on the Round Pond winery terrace overlooking Rutherford and Napa Valley.

TOP: Industrial, rustic chic was the focus of the MacDonnell family when designing the hospitality space at the Round Pond tasting room.

ABOVE: Owners Ryan and Miles MacDonnell.
Photographs by M. J. Wickham

FACING PAGE: *Photographs by M. J. Wickham*

ESTATE CABERNET SAUVIGNON

GOURMET PAIRINGS

The ideal pairing is estate chef Eric Maczko's creation of braised wild boar sliders with tomato confit, garlic emulsion, and mezuna. The various fats complement and amplify the wine's richness.

TASTING NOTES

Initial top notes of Spanish lavender and brambles give way to graphite, Asian plum, and cassis, followed by inviting fragrances of burnt vanilla caramel. The palate is balanced in its weighty structure. Round, well framed tannins encompass a plush core of mixed berry compote. The flavors are reminiscent of mocha-dusted baker's chocolate and dark cherries.

WINEMAKER'S INSIGHT

Sourced entirely from the three ranches that make up Round Pond Estate, this wine is meant to be a reflection of the terroir and vintage. The Estate Cabernet Sauvignon is the cornerstone of our wine portfolio and what wine lovers identify as the signature Round Pond taste. It is a wine crafted to be sophisticated yet unpretentious through thoughtful site selection, diligent vineyard management, and respectful handling in the cellar. The winemaking team focuses on maintaining ultra-premium quality in the Estate Cabernet Sauvignon.

TECHNICAL DATA

APPELLATION: Rutherford
COMPOSITION: 94% cabernet sauvignon, 5% petit verdot, 1% malbec
MATURATION: Aged for 19 months in 70% new, tight-grain French oak
CELLARING: Will peak six to 14 years from vintage
WEBSITE: www.roundpond.com

WATCH A VIDEO

Vintner Miles MacDonnell explains how Round Pond's Estate Cabernet Sauvignon mirrors the excellence of the estate, the temperate seasons, and the Napa Valley.

Shafer Vineyards NAPA

The name Shafer Vineyards calls to mind world-class Stags Leap District cabernet sauvignon. It's also the result of founder John Shafer's quest for a hillside vineyard—and his choice has proven fruitful in every way. Today John, his son Doug, and winemaker Elias Fernandez collaborate to create rich, elegant cabernet sauvignon, merlot, syrah, and chardonnay. In the early 1970s, John—convinced that the best wines came from grapes grown on rugged slopes—came to California to find the perfect hilly terrain. He discovered a 209-acre Napa site at the foot of the Stags Leap palisades; 30 acres of it had been planted to vines 50 years before. He also learned that

ABOVE: The winery offers a tasting experience that's relaxed and personable.

FACING PAGE: Shafer Vineyards sits at the heart of Stags Leap District.
Photographs by Russ Widstrand

HILLSIDE SELECT CABERNET SAUVIGNON

GOURMET PAIRINGS
The wine tastes perfect as a complement to chargrilled lamb cutlets with garlic-roasted kipfler potatoes and braised golden shallots.

TASTING NOTES
Hillside Select offers aromatic elegance and classic Stags Leap District flavors of black fruit, mocha, black plums, cassis, juicy black and red cherry, and black tea, with spice and warm toast. Ripe, silken tannins result in a pleasing, lengthy finish, smooth texture, and a refined structure, which offers the potential for very long-term aging.

WINEMAKER'S INSIGHT
Made of 100-percent cabernet sauvignon fruit sourced from rugged hillside vineyard blocks on our Stags Leap District estate, it's truly a "wine of place." The cabernet exemplifies the extraordinary richness and suppleness consistently produced in our little valley within a valley. It spends four full years aging: three in Alliers and Tronçais 100-percent new French oak barrels and one in the bottle.

TECHNICAL DATA

APPELLATION: Stags Leap District
COMPOSITION: 100% cabernet sauvignon
MATURATION: Aged 32 months in French oak and 15 months in bottle
CELLARING: Enjoyable today but will gain richness and maturity over the next 20 years
WEBSITE: www.shafervineyards.com

LEARN MORE

Learn more about Shafer Vineyards.

grapes had been growing on the land since the 1880s. In 1973, John and his family moved from Chicago to Napa to get on with his dream of planting hillside cabernet grapes; by 1978 it was time to harvest them to craft the first Shafer Vineyards wine, released in 1981 to high praise. Stags Leap District is an appellation that was formed in 1989 after John had organized a petition with neighboring grapegrowers and winery proprietors. The volcanic soil over weathered bedrock of the vineyard, and the scant rainfall, means the vines scramble for nutrients and produce small, concentrated berries rich in flavor. Delicious wines arising from gorgeous terroir—that's Shafer Vineyards.

ABOVE LEFT: The vineyards team harvests the fruit at night to ensure optimal flavors at the crush pad.

TOP: Hillside Select and the other wines age in French oak for a rich, flavorful finish.

ABOVE: John and Doug Shafer have worked side-by-side since 1983 as part of a partnership that has resulted in some of Napa Valley's most iconic wines.
Photographs by Russ Widstrand

FACING PAGE: *Photographs by Russ Widstrand*

Sherwin Family Vineyards ST. HELENA

Steven and Linda Sherwin were looking for a quieter, more relaxed setting than the Bay Area to raise their three children. A series of weekend visits to Napa Valley in 1996 uncovered a 30-acre property near the top of Spring Mountain with a beautiful home and serene lake. The real prize was the two acres of mixed old-vine cabernet sauvignon, merlot, and cabernet franc, originally part of a huge estate producing sought-after grapes in the late 1800s. With a contractor's hands-on approach, Steve cleared and planted 14 more acres, maintaining the same "field blend" ratio as the original vineyard and named the vineyard blocks for their three children: Jenny, Lindsey, and Matthew. Sherwin Family Vineyards released its first wine in 1999, from the 1996 vintage.

ABOVE: The tasting room patio overlooks the vineyards.

FACING PAGE: Sherwin Family Vineyards sit at the top of Spring Mountain.
Photographs by M. J. Wickham

Community minded and deeply patriotic, Sherwin Family Vineyards has become widely known as the "Home of the Patriotic Pour." The Sherwins created a very special bottle featuring the American flag—each hand-painted and numbered—to benefit the families of those lost on September 11. Sherwin Family Vineyards continues to donate these bottles to various charitable causes, as well as offers them to customers at the winery.

ABOVE LEFT: Sherwin Family Vineyards commemorative American flag bottle.

TOP: Proprietors Steven and Linda Sherwin with their trusty companion, Levi.

ABOVE: Sherwin Family Vineyards' tasting room.
Photographs by M. J. Wickham

FACING PAGE LEFT: *Photograph © iStockphoto.com/NightAndDayImages*
FACING PAGE RIGHT: *Photograph by M. J. Wickham*

ESTATE CABERNET SAUVIGNON

GOURMET PAIRINGS
A thick, juicy grilled ribeye steak with all the trimmings is the perfect pairing.

TASTING NOTES
With lush fruit notes and intensity thanks to its mountaintop growing conditions, the wine boasts hints of mocha, creamy oak, cassis, ripe currant, black cherry, and wild berry fruit. The well-integrated tannins combine with the flavors to create an elegant and stylish wine with a long, deep finish.

WINEMAKER'S INSIGHT
Marked by the firm backbone of Spring Mountain fruit, the Sherwin Family Vineyards Estate Cabernet Sauvignon exhibits the density, concentration, and intense flavors of the appellation.

TECHNICAL DATA

APPELLATION: Spring Mountain District
COMPOSITION: 80% cabernet sauvignon, 12% merlot, 8% cabernet franc
MATURATION: 20 months in new French oak, then six months in bottle
CELLARING: Exquisite upon release, best during its first six to eight years
WEBSITE: www.sherwinfamilyvineyards.com

WATCH A VIDEO

Steve Sherwin, proprietor of Sherwin Family Vineyards, describes his land and the Estate Cabernet Sauvignon, a wine that speaks for itself.

Signorello Estate   NAPA

Signorello Estate began as a father-son joint venture: Ray Signorello purchased 100 Napa acres for a vineyard in the mid-1970s and worked with his son, Ray Jr., to draw quality grapes from the land. The original plan involved acting as a grape grower for neighboring wineries. However, a bountiful 1985 harvest changed that by providing enough excess fruit for the Signorellos to try a crush of their own. The discovery that the grapes could become fantastic wine led to plans for a winery, built in 1986, and an expansion from vineyard into estate winery.

ABOVE: The eastern-facing rocky hillside vineyards produce distinctive cabernet fruit unique to the estate.

FACING PAGE: Signorello Estate overlooks the scenic Silverado Trail and Napa Valley.
Photographs by M. J. Wickham

PADRONE

GOURMET PAIRINGS
We recommend any favorite cut of high quality beef—roasted, braised, or grilled—as a pairing. Throw in the earthiness from some roasted wild mushrooms, and it's a perfect meal.

TASTING NOTES
The reticent nose opens to boysenberry, mulberry, vanilla, tobacco, and hints of chocolate. The lush, full-bodied palate continues with flavors of boysenberry, raspberry, cedar, and hints of vanilla. The young, integrated tannins accentuate the long and lingering finish.

WINEMAKER'S INSIGHT
Padrone is dedicated to Ray Signorello Sr., a visionary whose dreams became reality through our wines, which are as full of character as his life. A fitting tribute to the life of Ray Sr., Padrone is a wine that expresses the quality and dignity of the winery. We source the grapes from two extremely rocky parts of our estate vineyard with yields of only 1.3 tons per acre.

TECHNICAL DATA

APPELLATION: Napa Valley
COMPOSITION: 84% cabernet sauvignon, 8% merlot, 8% cabernet franc
MATURATION: Aged for 20 months in 70% new Tronçais, Nevers, and Allier oak
CELLARING: Cellar for 10-plus years
WEBSITE: www.signorelloestate.com

WATCH A VIDEO

Watch a video of proprietor Ray Signorello Jr. explaining the nuances of Signorello Estate's Padrone, a rich Bordeaux-style blend.

The romantic aspects of winemaking—good food, good wine, a gorgeous setting—originally attracted the Signorellos to Napa. Of course there is labor too, but Signorello Estate turns that into an art through the philosophy of the vigneron: the winemaker who begins his work at the vine. This technique, prevalent in the Bordeaux region of France, produces wines with elegance and balance. Ray Jr. and winemaker Pierre Birebent pay special attention to every step of the winemaking process, from the barrels to bottling, and each grape varietal receives a different careful treatment. From magnificent cabernet sauvignons to elegant chardonnays to premium standouts Padrone and Hope's Cuvée, all strive to emulate those crafted by the top châteaux of Bordeaux and Burgundy.

ABOVE LEFT: The private dining room offers an elegant setting for food and wine pairings.

TOP: Originally built in 1985, the tasting room provides a sophisticated environment for sampling limited production wines grown, produced, and bottled on the estate.

ABOVE: Sweeping views of Napa Valley provide a relaxing atmosphere for guests to enjoy handcrafted wines.
Photographs by M. J. Wickham

FACING PAGE LEFT: *Photograph by M. J. Wickham*
FACING PAGE RIGHT: *Photograph courtesy of Signorello Estate*

Silver Oak Cellars OAKVILLE

Exceptionally wonderful cabernet sauvignon that is perfectly drinkable upon release: that's the sole focus of Silver Oak Cellars, which provides its faithful consumers with great wines that hail from some of the best cabernet vineyards of Napa Valley and Alexander Valley. Entrepreneur Raymond Duncan founded the winery in 1972 with Justin Meyer on the premise that the winery would dedicate itself to one varietal and submit to an extensive barreling and aging process. Today the name Silver Oak is synonymous with exceptional cabernet, and the family-owned legacy continues as Raymond has passed the torch to his sons David and Tim to

ABOVE: The tasting room entrance of Silver Oak's Oakville winery.
Photograph by Adrian Gregorutti

FACING PAGE: The iconic water tower of Silver Oak Cellars.
Photograph by M. J. Wickham

NAPA VALLEY CABERNET SAUVIGNON

GOURMET PAIRINGS
Winery chef Dominic Orsini suggests pairing vine-grilled Wagyu beef striploin with braised shortrib with a porcini mushroom cannelloni. The dish suggests a forest floor aroma that enhances the wine's earthy character.

TASTING NOTES
The wine combines the rich blackberry and cassis character of cabernet sauvignon with the velvety black cherry character of merlot from our Soda Canyon Ranch, the violet notes of cabernet franc, and the high notes of petit verdot. Top-quality American oak from our partners at A&K Cooperage in Missouri imparts a sandalwood characteristic.

WINEMAKER'S INSIGHT
Our wines aim to be profound and age well, expressing ripe fruit character at moderate alcohol. We source fruit from a number of properties throughout the Napa Valley appellation. Our wine is blended prior to barreling and then aged for 24 months in 100-percent new American oak before laying down for an additional 20 months in bottle to further harmonize flavors before release.

TECHNICAL DATA

APPELLATION: Napa Valley
COMPOSITION: 90% cabernet, 6% merlot, 3% petit verdot, 1% cabernet franc
MATURATION: 24 months in 100% new American oak barrel, 20 months in bottle
CELLARING: Deliciously drinkable upon release, but proper cellaring allows for further complexity and enjoyment
WEBSITE: www.silveroak.com

LEARN MORE

Learn more about Silver Oak Cellars.

direct the future of one of Napa Valley's most iconic wineries.

The goal at Silver Oak has always been to capture the unique and powerful terroir of the well regarded and highly sought-after Alexander and Napa Valley appellations. Winemaker Daniel Baron meticulously evaluates and selects grapes from vineyards which exhibit the characteristics essential to Silver Oak wines. A special blending process occurs prior to barreling, which allows the wine to fully harmonize before the winery's hallmark American oak exerts its spiced

TOP: Silver Oak's glass cellar.
Photograph by Adrian Gregorutti

LEFT: The covered patio overlooks the vineyards at the Oakville winery.
Photograph by Adrian Gregorutti

RIGHT: The state-of-the-art winery.
Photograph by M. J. Wickham

FACING PAGE LEFT: *Photograph by Sara Sanger*
FACING PAGE RIGHT: *Photograph by M. J. Wickham*

influence. The end result is supremely expressive and rich wines that are a hit with consumers and critics alike. A turning point came in 2006, when a fire devastated the winery. Tragedy was turned into opportunity as the Duncan family set out to build a new winery from scratch, making use of all the experience the team had accumulated over the previous 35 years. In addition to recreating the timelessly grand American architectural style—in homage to the dairy once on the site—the team brought in stone reclaimed from an abandoned Kansas flour mill to restore and expand the property. The winemaking, bottling, and cellaring operations then received numerous technological updates to provide the winemaking team with the best tools possible to craft their cabernet. In the end, the fire strengthened not only the winery but also tasters' appetites for Silver Oak's celebrated cabernet.

TOP: Office and meeting spaces at Silver Oak Cellars.

MIDDLE: The barrel chai.

BOTTOM: The tasting room.

FACING PAGE: The event chai leading into the winery at Silver Oak.
Photographs by M. J. Wickham

Silverado Vineyards   NAPA

In 1880, local writer Robert Louis Stevenson likened the beginning of vine planting to the beginning of precious metal mining: the vine grower is just as much of a prospector as the miner. A century later, the Miller family began the journey Stevenson described, establishing Silverado Vineyards in 1981 on two parcels of producing vineyard land along the Silverado Trail, in what is now known as the Stags Leap District. With the land came contracts for selling grapes to some of Napa's best vintners, and the family continued to do so until they decided to build their own beautiful winery on the property. In the following years, the Millers continued to "prospect" as they added Miller Ranch, Mount George, Soda Canyon, and two Carneros vineyards to their original property holdings, each with their own

ABOVE: The Stags Leap Vineyard.
Photograph by Terence Ford

FACING PAGE: The entrance to the winery's tasting room.
Photograph courtesy of Silverado Vineyards

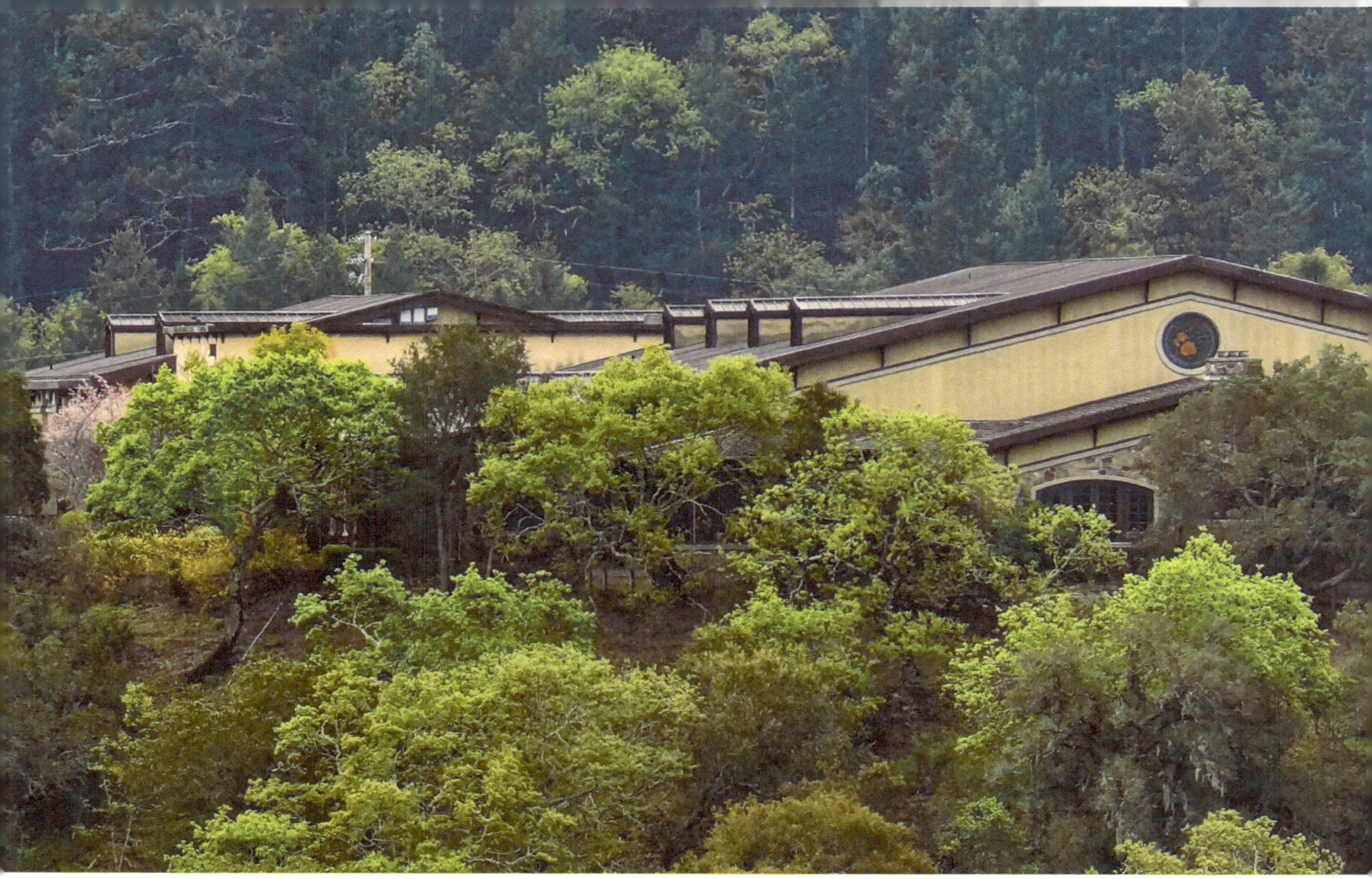

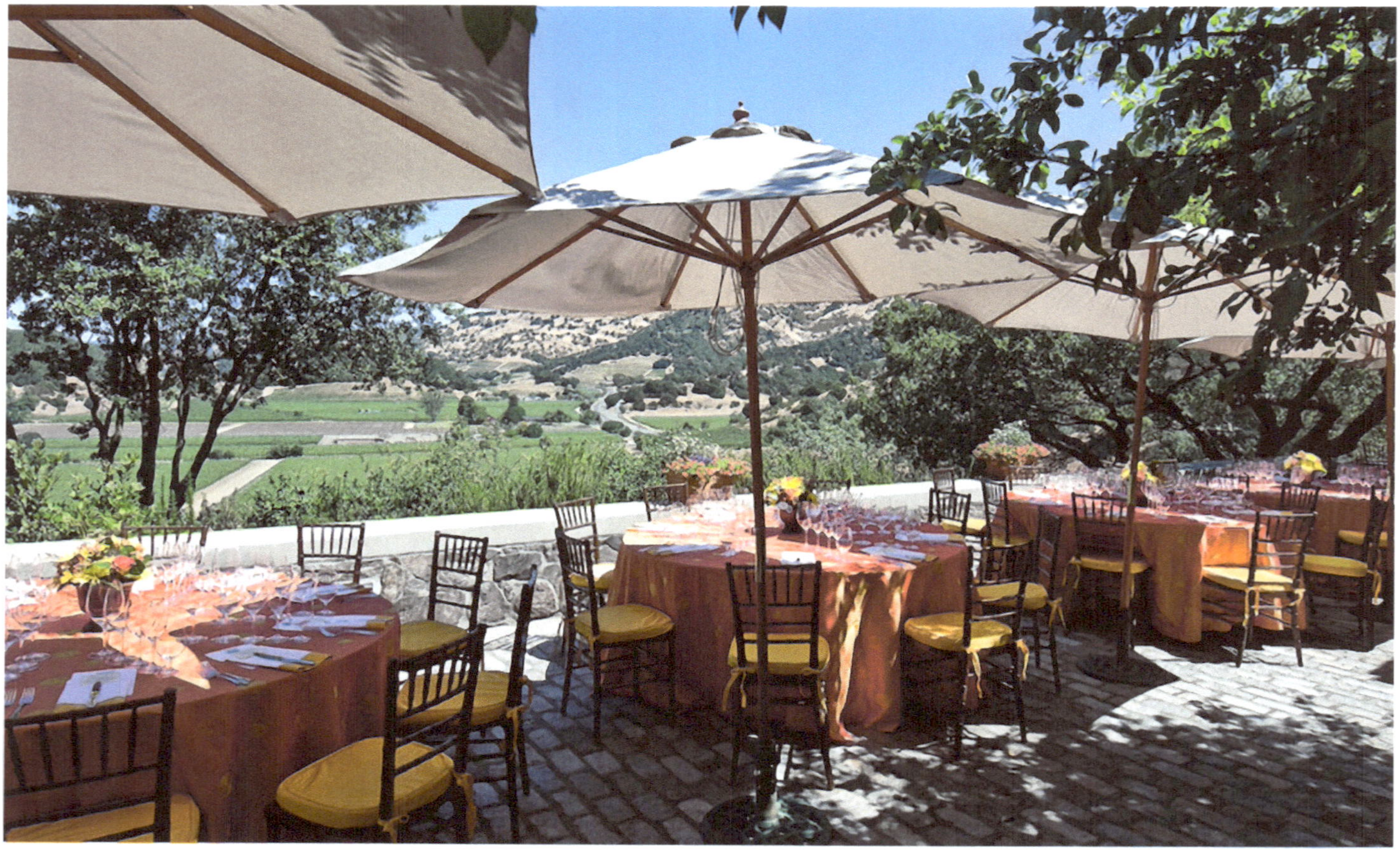

distinctive character.

Today the winery honors the uniqueness and quality of these vineyards by producing limited bottlings from each appellation. Under the direction and guidance of general manager Russ Weis and winemaker Jon Emmerich—only the second winemaker in the winery's history—Silverado offers an array of single varietal wines and red blends including cabernet sauvignon, merlot, sauvignon blanc, chardonnay, sangiovese, zinfandel, and malbec. The winery, known for its majestic view,

ABOVE: The hilltop winery provides sweeping views of the valley below.
Photograph by Peter Bowers

RIGHT: The illustration on the bottle's label is by Annabelle Miller, Ron and Diane's granddaughter.
Photograph by Christine Tomlinson

FACING PAGE BOTTOM: Silverado Vineyards offers tours and is a great location for private and club member events.
Photograph by Allan Ezial

is a beautiful setting in which to sample the wines and enjoy a broad range of tour and tasting experiences. For the Millers, sustainable means more than just a way to farm. It is the governing approach to all their activities at the winery—from land preservation to solar power to creating lasting, quality relationships with their neighbors—which ensures that the estate and winery will remain in Napa for years to come.

ABOVE: Three generations of the Miller family.
Photograph by Avis Mandel

LEFT: The upper terrace on a tranquil afternoon.
Photograph by Peter Bowers

FACING PAGE LEFT: *Photograph © iStockphoto.com/hlphoto*
FACING PAGE RIGHT: *Photograph courtesy of Silverado Vineyards*

SOLO CABERNET SAUVIGNON

GOURMET PAIRINGS
Pair with grilled duck breast with sautéed fresh cherries, arugula, and balsamic reduction, or braised Angus shortribs and white Cheddar pearl tapioca.

TASTING NOTES
A classic example of Stags Leap cabernet, the wine is elegant and well balanced. Aromas of raspberry, black cherry, and plum dance against earth and herb notes. With a medium body, the wine boasts a broad mid-palate of lush, perfectly ripe fruit.

WINEMAKER'S INSIGHT
The wine comes from the Silverado's Stags Leap Vineyard, which stretches between the Silverado Trail and the Napa River and is made up primarily of Silverado's own indigenous clone, the UC Davis Silverado Disney Heritage Clone #30. The vineyard produces complex, ripe fruit with supple texture and solid structure, evident in every bottle of SOLO.

TECHNICAL DATA
COMPOSITION: 100% cabernet sauvignon
MATURATION: Aged 19 months in 100% French oak barrels
CELLARING: May be cellared up to 15 to 20 years
WEBSITE: www.silveradovineyards.com

LEARN MORE

Learn more about Silverado Vineyards.

Spring Mountain Vineyard   ST. HELENA

Founded in 1873, Spring Mountain Vineyard has left its mark on Napa Valley as one of the region's founding wineries. Its oldest vineyard, La Perla, holds the distinction of growing the first cabernet sauvignon vines on Spring Mountain. Today this family-owned and sustainably-farmed winery encompasses four contiguous historic vineyards that have been combined into one 845-acre estate. While known for its Bordeaux-style blend and cabernet, it was initially acclaimed for its chardonnay when it placed fourth at the 1976 Judgment of Paris tasting, beating out numerous established Burgundy wines. Spring Mountain grows cabernet sauvignon, the complementary red Bordeaux varieties, chardonnay, sauvignon blanc, and pinot noir.

ABOVE: A century-old olive tree frames a serene Spring Mountain landscape, with gobelet-trained vines, steep terraces, and a 1886 Eastlake-style horse barn.
Photograph by Nwm Arts

FACING PAGE: The 1974 winery is built into the hillside and leads to 19th-century wine caves.
Photograph by M. J. Wickham

The vineyard comprises 225 acres of the estate and is separated into 135 separate blocks, which rise from 400 to 1,600 feet in elevation. With diverse microclimates, exposures, and soil types, the vineyard is situated above the fog line and enjoys long days of sunshine with moderate temperature variation. It yields smaller grapes of rich color and concentrated flavor, high residual acidity, and supple tannins that, under the direction of the owner—a European wine connoisseur and collector—produce unique and high-quality Bordeaux-style wines. Each vineyard block is harvested by hand and fermented and barreled separately until blending.

ABOVE: A dramatic look through time; new French oak fermentation vessels mark the entrance to 19th- and 20th-century caves where estate wines age before bottling.
Photograph by M. J. Wickham

RIGHT: The towers of the 1891 Chateau Chevalier are surrounded by cabernet vines.
Photograph by Nwm Arts

FACING PAGE LEFT: *Photograph © iStockphoto.com/NightAndDayImages*
FACING PAGE RIGHT: *Photograph by M. J. Wickham*

ELIVETTE

GOURMET PAIRINGS

Roasted tenderloin of beef with a mushroom and red wine reduction complements the layered nuances of Elivette, Spring Mountain Vineyard's signature Bordeaux-style wine.

TASTING NOTES

Seductive aromas of bright red fruit, cedar, cinnamon, and cola mingle with toasty notes of fine French oak. The palate is soft, elegant, and lush, redolent with Spring Mountain's classic red cherry core. A lingering finish that glides across the palate suggests a rewarding future.

WINEMAKER'S INSIGHT

Like all of our wines, Elivette is estate bottled so we can direct every step of the process from vine to glass. Our vineyards give us a beautiful palette of wines to choose from at blending time. To create Elivette, we marry the lots with exceptional structure and elegance into an age-worthy wine.

TECHNICAL DATA

APPELLATION: Spring Mountain District
COMPOSITION: 55% cabernet sauvignon, 22% cabernet franc, 12% petit verdot, 10% merlot, 1% malbec
MATURATION: 22 months in new French oak
CELLARING: Elivette will cellar for decades of enjoyment
WEBSITE: www.springmountainvineyard.com

WATCH A VIDEO

Learn about Spring Mountain Vineyard's flagship wine, a Bordeaux blend comprised of distinctive, estate-grown grapes from winemaker Jac Cole.

ESTATE BOTTLED CABERNET SAUVIGNON

GOURMET PAIRINGS

A simple, grilled ribeye steak or lamb chop is terrific with Spring Mountain Cabernet Sauvignon. The wine's chewy tannins and bright acidity refresh the palate after each bite.

TASTING NOTES

Effusive aromas of sweet dark fruit, cocoa, caramel, and intriguing notes of violets introduce the wine. The mid-palate is laden with intense fruit—blackberry, raspberry, and cassis—and is further enhanced by notes of chocolate and baking spices. The finish is long and lingering, restating the fruit and spice elements.

WINEMAKER'S INSIGHT

All of our wines are estate bottled. We direct every step of the process, from vine to glass. Our cabernet sauvignon is a rich and concentrated wine that reflects its mountainside origin.

TECHNICAL DATA

APPELLATION: Spring Mountain District
COMPOSITION: 86% cabernet sauvignon, 12% cabernet franc, 2% merlot
MATURATION: 22 months in new French oak
CELLARING: To fully appreciate its complexity, decant the wine while young
WEBSITE: www.springmountainvineyard.com

WATCH A VIDEO

Winemaker Jac Cole examines how the vineyard's terroir creates many different expressions of cabernet.

While the estate's topography presents a farming challenge for vineyard manager Ron Rosenbrand, its diversity gives winemaker Jac Cole a unique and rich palette from which to choose specific profile characteristics and create nuanced and refined wines. Together Ron and Jac select specific rootstocks and clones best suited to the terroir, determine the balance of vine canopy for fruit maturation and, in the autumn, evaluate the perfect point of harvest of each vineyard block. The legacy started at the Judgment of Paris continues today at Spring Mountain Vineyard with the production of wines that reflect the spirit of Bordeaux and the soul of Napa Valley.

ABOVE: Deep in the recesses of the wine caves, a candlelit tasting awaits.

RIGHT: The sculpted terraces of the Chevalier Vineyard were established in the 1880s by Fortune Chevalier.
Photographs by M. J. Wickham

FACING PAGE LEFT: *Photograph by M. J. Wickham*
FACING PAGE RIGHT: *Photograph © iStockphoto.com/evgenyb*

Staglin Family Vineyard — RUTHERFORD

At Staglin Family Vineyard, all four members of the family work together closely day by day to produce varietal wines of distinction. Shari and Garen Staglin founded the winery in 1985 after years of study, and later welcomed children Brandon and Shannon to the fold as full-fledged winery team members. Son of Pasquale Stagliano—naturalized to Ramon Staglin—Garen has an Italian heritage and upbringing that made wine a part of life from an early age. During the 1960s, Garen and Shari visited Napa often, and frequented local wine shops in Washington, D.C. and New York City before moving to Northern California. By 1985, a dream finally came true:

ABOVE: The historic Steckter House, originally built in 1864.
Photograph by M. J. Wickham

FACING PAGE: Situated at the base of the western slope of Mount St. John, the tallest mountain in the Mayacamas Range, the 61-acre property is located in an alluvial fan containing rich volcanic soils.
Photograph by Andy Berry, Purkinje Blue

ESTATE CABERNET SAUVIGNON

GOURMET PAIRINGS
The wine pairs perfectly with lamb chops on a golden bed of polenta, vineyard mustard greens, wild mushrooms, and a Staglin cabernet reduction sauce.

TASTING NOTES
The wine has an archetypal Old World sauvignon nose laden with classic aromas of cassis, black cherry, and redolent with violet-lifted black olives and green peppercorns. The aromas cascade onto a rich and vibrant palate of anise-highlighted blackcurrants and peppered plums. Tingly notes of powdered minerals and a fresh acidity combine to give length to the well-formed tannins.

WINEMAKER'S INSIGHT
Certified organic farming practices characterize the grape growing process and enhance fruit and wine quality. The vineyard crew thins the clusters two to four times during each growing season to balance each vine. The clusters that remain get more nutrients and grow grapes with optimal flavor. Adding multiple clone and rootstock combinations to each vineyard block increases biodiversity and flavor complexity.

TECHNICAL DATA

APPELLATION: Rutherford
COMPOSITION: 88% cabernet sauvignon, 8% cabernet franc, 4% petit verdot
MATURATION: 22 months
CELLARING: Drink now or cellar for up to 10 years
WEBSITE: www.staglinfamily.com

WATCH A VIDEO

Co-proprieter Shari Staglin names the flavors, strengths, and characteristics of Staglin Family Vineyard's flagship wine, cabernet sauvignon.

the family acquired 64 total acres of land.

The Staglin Family Vineyard label was founded on the values of family ownership, commitment to quality, and memorable experiences for guests and tasters. Brandon and Shannon grew up on the property and joined their parents' business as adults after gaining valuable experience and education elsewhere.

Of the acreage purchased in 1985, the majority had first been planted in 1868 as part of the historic Steckter

TOP: 2011 Staglin Family Vineyard cabernet sauvignon grapes.
Photograph by Andy Berry, Purkinje Blue

ABOVE: Shannon, Garen, Shari, and Brandon Staglin.
Photograph by M. J. Wickham

LEFT: Under the expert guidance of vineyard manager David Abreu and foreman Richard Villaseñor, the crew meticulously cares for the organic vineyard year-round.
Photograph by Kopol Bonick Studios

FACING PAGE: *Photographs by M. J. Wickham*

estate. In 2007, the Staglins were able to acquire the original Steckter home that once stood next to the vineyards. Today the team of vineyard manager David Abreu, winemaker Fredrik Johansson, and consulting winemaker Michel Rolland guide the vines and wines to excellence. Biodiversity, 100-percent organic farming, and running on 100-percent solar power result in healthy vineyards at no extra cost to the environment. The 24,000-square-foot underground production facility, equipped with modern caves, furthers the minimized ecological impact.

Philanthropy also comes into play at Staglin. All proceeds from the wines made under the Salus label go to fundraising for mental health research. Respect for the land and for humanity alike—that's the conscientious attitude that contributes in no small part to Staglin Family Vineyard's wonderful cabernet sauvignon, chardonnay, sangiovese, and Bordeaux blend offerings.

TOP: Completed in 2002, the 24,000-square-foot underground production facility is customized to enhance the unique characteristics of the vineyard.

MIDDLE: Winemaker Fredrik Johansson utilizes both stainless and wooden tanks for fermentations and macerations.

BOTTOM: The modern caves provide naturally gentle storage conditions with a cool constant temperature and mild humidity.

FACING PAGE: The Steckter House salon set for an elegant dinner with beautiful views of Napa Valley.
Photographs by M. J. Wickham

Trefethen Family Vineyards   NAPA

In 1968, when concrete seemed to be creeping its way into the rolling hills of farmland and threatening to encroach on the slopes of Napa, Eugene Trefethen and his wife Catherine purchased seven farms surrounding a gorgeous but rundown 19th-century winery in southern Napa Valley, hoping to leave a more agrarian legacy for their family. Son John diverged from his parents' original plan to sell the grapes produced at Trefethen; he and his wife Janet—who founded the Oak Knoll District appellation—produced the winery's first vintage in 1973. In three short years, Trefethen Family Vineyards went from being a freshman winery to an award-wining establishment: the 1976 Chardonnay earned Best Chardonnay in the World honors at the 1979 Gault Millau World Wine Olympics in Paris.

ABOVE: Designated a National Historic Landmark, Trefethen's 19th-century redwood winery is still a working cellar and home to its world-renowned tasting room.
Photograph by Andy Katz

FACING PAGE: A classic wine estate, Trefethen Family Vineyards is encircled by vineyards and sweeping views of the surrounding Napa Valley hills.
Photograph by M. J. Wickham

From those early, accolade-filled years, the winery has passed to the third generation of Trefethens and has continued to influence the Napa industry. John and Janet's children, Loren and Hailey, assist their parents in the operation of the family-centered enterprise. Janet, along with mother-in-law Catherine and several other female vintners, was instrumental in influencing the trend of food and wine pairings in Napa. Trefethen has also become a leader in sustainable grape growing, adopting environmentally conscious methods for growing its array of varietals: riesling, chardonnay, pinot noir, cabernet franc, merlot, malbec, cabernet sauvignon, viognier, and petit verdot.

Never having purchased outside grapes to make their wines, the Trefethens are committed to being good stewards of the land, responsible neighbors, and enlightened employers. The award-winning wines—including the 2005 Reserve Cabernet Sauvignon, which was named the Wine of the Year by *Wine Enthusiast* magazine—are produced from grapes harvested in early morning, grown in vineyards tucked away from busy life—the epitome of Eugene Trefethen's dream.

ABOVE: Located in the first floor of the winery, guests see firsthand how wines are aged in the wine cellar.

TOP RIGHT: The tasting room offers a warm, comfortable environment in which to sample Trefethen's distinctive and award-winning wines.

RIGHT: The entrance to the tasting room is filled with antique winery equipment and photos of the historic building through the ages.
Photographs by M. J. Wickham

FACING PAGE: *Photographs by M. J. Wickham*

HĀLO CABERNET SAUVIGNON

GOURMET PAIRINGS
The subtle tones of smoke pair well with pan-seared beef tenderloin, baby kale, black trumpet mushrooms, and tomato confit. Ripe tomatoes, herbs, and fresh ground black pepper accentuate the palate of the wine.

TASTING NOTES
Aromas of blackberries and bay leaves—like those that grow along the spring-fed creek that flows through the Hillspring property—flow through HāLo. Subtle notes of oak, tobacco, smoke, and earth, derived from the soil itself, dance in the background of the wine. With flavors of cassis, black cherry, dark chocolate, and juicy plum, the wine boasts ripe, refined tannins.

WINEMAKER'S INSIGHT
Named for third-generation Trefethens Hailey and Loren, HāLo is our flagship wine. Grown in our Hillspring Vineyard in the Mayacamas foothills of western Napa Valley, the grapes come from shallow soils, a protected climate, and a long growing season—the perfect combination for fine crops of cabernet sauvignon.

TECHNICAL DATA

APPELLATION: Oak Knoll District
COMPOSITION: 92% cabernet sauvignon, 5% petit verdot, 3% malbec
MATURATION: 28 months in French oak barrels
CELLARING: The wine is designed for long-term aging of more than 20 years
WEBSITE: www.trefethen.com

WATCH A VIDEO

Loren Trefethen explains how HāLo Cabernet Sauvignon represents the future of Trefethen Family Vineyards.

HARMONY CHARDONNAY

GOURMET PAIRINGS

The wine pairs beautifully with macadamia nut-encrusted halibut with coconut corn purée and piquillo pepper coulis. Sweet vegetables and succulent seafood play beautifully against the wine's citrus aromas.

TASTING NOTES

Bright golden yellow in color, the aromas range from peach to lemon meringue and butterscotch. In the mouth, the classic Trefethen brightness is framed by a very full body, resulting from the time spent sur lie. With a kiss of oak, the wine has a long, persistent, and utterly seductive finish.

WINEMAKER'S INSIGHT

Grown from a special section of our estate vineyard known as Katie's Acre, the wine is produced from a combination of four different chardonnay clones—two recent imports from France and two selections with a long heritage in California.

TECHNICAL DATA

APPELLATION: Oak Knoll District
COMPOSITION: 100% chardonnay
MATURATION: 11 months in 20% new French oak barrels
CELLARING: Trefethen chardonnays are designed to cellar for 10-plus years
WEBSITE: www.trefethen.com

WATCH A VIDEO

Hailey Trefethen talks about the origins of Harmony Chardonnay, including its history and qualities.

TOP: Founder Katie Trefethen was an avid gardener and has left a legacy of beautiful landscapes surrounding the estate.

ABOVE: The third generation of Trefethens, Loren and Hailey, grew up playing on the Trefethen estates and in the Hillspring Vineyard.

LEFT: A secret passage leads to over five acres of flowers, fruits, and vegetables for use by Trefethen employees—a long-standing company benefit.
Photographs by M. J. Wickham

FACING PAGE: *Photographs by M. J. Wickham*

Twomey Cellars   CALISTOGA

In 1999, members of the Silver Oak family decided to take their nearly 30 years of winemaking expertise and branch out into varietals outside of their famed cabernet sauvignon under the label Twomey Cellars. Named after Silver Oak co-founder Raymond Twomey Duncan's mother Velma Twomey, and in honor of a proud Irish heritage, Twomey Cellars produces estate, appellation, and single-vineyard merlot, pinot noir, and sauvignon blanc. Twomey began with the harvest of merlot from Silver Oak's Soda Canyon Ranch in 1999. Silver Oak winemaker Daniel Baron, well versed in the artistry of merlot, recognized the opportunity to craft a world-class wine with Old World techniques.

ABOVE: The Twomey Cellars winery in Calistoga.
Photograph by Robb McDonough

FACING PAGE: The winery and its grounds.
Photograph by M. J. Wickham

NAPA VALLEY MERLOT

GOURMET PAIRINGS
Winery chef Dominic Orsini recommends wild nettle spaghetti with lamb meatballs, preserved Meyer lemon, olives, and mint. The herbaceous aromas and lemons' bright contrast complement the merlot.

TASTING NOTES
Merlot, at its finest, has a velvety texture with explosive aromas of black cherry and blackberry, with notes of tar and roasted game. To achieve these characteristics, we source exclusively from our ideally located Soda Canyon Ranch and apply the classic soutirage traditionnel technique. A small amount of cabernet franc adds elements of violets and roasted coffee to the refined and focused wine.

WINEMAKER'S INSIGHT
On Soda Canyon Ranch's rolling hills of volcanic soil, we grow French merlot clones specifically chosen for their yields of small, intensely flavored berries. After harvest, wine ages in thin-staved French oak barrels as we employ soutirage traditionnel, a labor-intensive technique perfected by director of winemaking Daniel Baron during his tenure in Pomerol, France, that clarifies the wine and softens the tannins as it transfers from barrel to barrel.

TECHNICAL DATA

APPELLATION: Napa Valley
COMPOSITION: 95% merlot, 5% cabernet franc
MATURATION: 15 months in French barrels; three or four soutirages per vintage
CELLARING: Perfectly enjoyable upon release, with excellent cellaring potential
WEBSITE: www.twomey.com

LEARN MORE

Learn more about Twomey Cellars.

The acquisition of a pinot noir vineyard in the heart of the Russian River appellation a year later firmly established a journey toward new discovery with the first vintage being produced in 2002.

Today Twomey sources from only the best vineyard sites and the team enjoys the creative outlet offered by the venture. With one location in Calistoga—home to merlot production, where visitors are treated to a stylish, courtyard-adjacent tasting room with views of landscaped gardens and lush vineyards—and another in Healdsburg, where pinot noir and sauvignon blanc are produced, Twomey Cellars contributes to the Silver Oak family's impressive Northern California presence.

Above all, Twomey Cellars is proudly family-owned and operated; the Duncans, always in search of the best, possess an adventurous spirit drawn toward evolution and discovery, a spirit which is reflected in every bottle of Twomey wine.

ABOVE LEFT: The merlot is checked for clarity during soutirage traditionnel.

TOP: A pair of cyclists visits the winery in beautiful Calistoga.

ABOVE: The tasting room at Twomey Cellars.
Photographs by M. J. Wickham

FACING PAGE LEFT: *Photograph by Sara Sanger*
FACING PAGE RIGHT: *Photograph by M. J. Wickham*

Vineyard 7&8   ST. HELENA

The journey began in 1999, when Launny and Weezie Steffens purchased the 40-acre estate that is now Vineyard 7&8. Launny's passion for wine had led him to dream of crafting a fine wine of his own one day, so the existing vineyards on the property made it irresistible. The name nods to numbers of good fortune in both eastern and western cultures, and double as personal lucky numbers for Launny, a Wall Street financier. The couple's youngest son, Wesley, manages the daily operations while assisting winemaker Luc Morlet throughout the entire winemaking process. Trained as a chef and intrigued by the interaction of food and wine, Wesley began his career in wine with a four-year stint at Harlan Estate Winery, where he learned the craft of winemaking and eventually took on the role of cellarmaster.

ABOVE: The main entrance to the winery facility.

FACING PAGE: Sunrise over the estate chardonnay and cabernet vineyards high on Spring Mountain.
Photographs by M. J. Wickham

ESTATE CABERNET SAUVIGNON

GOURMET PAIRINGS
A grilled filet of beef simply seasoned with extra virgin olive oil, sea salt, and freshly ground pepper complements the structure and power of the wine. Pairs wonderfully with bittersweet chocolate bark with almonds and fleur de sel.

TASTING NOTES
Despite its youth, the opulent and rich wine is ready to be uncorked now, though it will age nicely for at least 15 years. Representative of other pure and authoritative Spring Mountain cabernets, oak flavors have been capably integrated to forge a full-bodied mouthfeel and a long finish. Notable characteristics include a ruby-purple color and a nose of wildflowers, berries, and blackcurrants.

WINEMAKER'S INSIGHT
The estate-only bottling of our cabernet sauvignon highlights the unique character of the special Vineyard 7&8 terroir. Planted back in the early 1980s, the mature vines of the estate benefit from white volcanic tuff well-drained soil, producing small, concentrated clusters and berries. The resulting lots of barrels displayed intensity, complexity, richness, and depth. Through each vintage, the estate wine represents the best the estate has to offer. Built to age gracefully for several decades, the estate cabernet is a memory of a very special place.

TECHNICAL DATA

APPELLATION: Spring Mountain District
COMPOSITION: 100% cabernet sauvignon
MATURATION: Aged 18 months in oak barrels
CELLARING: Approachable now and will age well
WEBSITE: www.vineyard7and8.com

WATCH A VIDEO

Watch a video of vintner Wesley Steffens delving into the intricacies of Vineyard 7&8's estate-grown cabernet sauvignon.

He ventured up Spring Mountain in 2006 to complete construction and take over daily management of the winery.

Vineyard 7&8 produces wine from just two varietals: cabernet sauvignon and chardonnay. Two of the wines come from estate-grown grapes; the other two come from fellow Spring Mountain and Russian River Valley sources. With a philosophy that remains simple yet focused, the winery strives to produce premium handcrafted wines that highlight a sense of place within the Spring Mountain District through experience, passion, and humility.

TOP: The "rotunda" tasting room highlights 180-degree views of the valley below.

ABOVE: Stainless steel tanks in the fermentation room.

LEFT: New French oak barrels prepped and ready for harvest.

FACING PAGE: *Photographs by M. J. Wickham*

Vineyard 29 ST. HELENA

"If you can't measure it, you can't improve it," is the guiding principle that Chuck McMinn embraced during 25 years in the high-tech startup industry. When he and his wife Anne moved to Napa Valley and acquired Vineyard 29 just north of St. Helena in 2000, they applied that principle to wine production as well, using advanced modern technologies as a compass to guide the application of Old World winemaking techniques. At Vineyard 29, the McMinns discovered that measurement not only leads to improvement of wines, it leads to transcendence. In just one decade, Chuck and Anne have propelled Vineyard 29's trajectory from a single vineyard planted by David Abreu to a full-scale, technologically unparalleled winery overseen by cabernet clairvoyant Philippe Melka.

ABOVE: The impressive front entrance to the winery.
FACING PAGE: The vineyards overlook Napa Valley.
Photographs by M. J. Wickham

29 ESTATE CABERNET SAUVIGNON

GOURMET PAIRINGS
Pair with seared New York strip, caramelized corn, and bacon with a red wine-thyme sauce from Vineyard 29's "Library Experience" tasting. The corn brings out sweet fruit tones while the bacon highlights smoky oak notes.

TASTING NOTES
The 29 Estate property continues to delight with wines of extraordinary elegance and sophistication. The 29 Estate Cabernet's elegance is defined by floral aromas of delicate rose petals with hints of minerality from warm crushed stone and graphite. Deep red fruits add lusciousness and lingering depth. On the palate, ripe red fruits, cracked black pepper, and exotic spices combine for a seemingly endless finish of this vibrant, complex, and expressive wine.

WINEMAKER'S INSIGHT
The most careful and patient—albeit time-consuming and labor-intensive—techniques create wines that fully express the potential of their vineyard heritage. Every cluster is hand-sorted, then a second sorting table allows 16 people to hand-sort each individual grape once it is de-stemmed. Whole grapes are deposited into a small transfer tank, which is then lifted by forklift so that the grapes may slide gently by gravity into computer-monitored fermentation tanks.

TECHNICAL DATA

APPELLATION: St. Helena
COMPOSITION: At least 95% cabernet sauvignon with cabernet franc and petit verdot
MATURATION: Aged in French oak barrels
CELLARING: Three years of bottle aging and decanting beneficial; cellar for 20 to 25 years
WEBSITE: www.vineyard29.com

WATCH A VIDEO

Watch a video of vintner Chuck McMinn describing the unique benefits of the Vineyard 29 terroir.

The first step the McMinns took toward expanding the winery's portfolio was the acquisition of the historic Aida vineyard in late 2000, as Aida proved to be the ideal complement to the already esteemed Vineyard 29 estate.

The next step was constructing a world-class winery that could utilize advanced technology to facilitate and buttress Old World winemaking practices. To achieve this, Chuck brought in highly regarded architect Jon Lail to partner with winemaker Philippe Melka on the design and construction of a 17,000-square-foot facility. Completed in 2003, the winery is a reflection of the marriage between Chuck's technology background and Philippe's traditional winemaking philosophy.

TOP: Vintner Chuck McMinn at the stunning entrance to Vineyard 29.
MIDDLE: The foyer has a welcoming design and modern art touches.
BOTTOM: The winery's interior contains a pristine row of stainless steel fermentation tanks.
Photographs by M. J. Wickham

FACING PAGE: *Photographs by M. J. Wickham*

With distinct vineyard sites, a state-of-the-art winemaking facility, and the unquestionable skill of winemaker Philippe Melka, all the stars aligned for Chuck and Anne to lead Vineyard 29 to a new and exciting level of winemaking. Today Vineyard 29 harnesses the full winemaking potential of its vineyards, caring for the fruit down to the single berry and crafting memorable wines from the soil up.

ABOVE: The wine caves, lined with French oak barrels, age future vintages of Vineyard 29 wines.

LEFT: The caves are as appealing to guests as they are perfect for aging wines, complete with a Chihuly room featuring his art. The wine library is the perfect place for a tasting experience.
Photographs by M. J. Wickham

FACING PAGE: *Photographs by M. J. Wickham*

29 ESTATE SAUVIGNON BLANC

GOURMET PAIRINGS
When tasted with a Gulf shrimp, mango, and Meyer lemon salad in a Vineyard 29 "Library Experience," the wine's crisp acidity cuts through the shrimp's richness, while the mango brings out the wine's tropical tones.

TASTING NOTES
The wine opens with complex and exquisite aromas of fresh crushed stone, bright lemon zest, and white peach. Gentle swirling brings out fleshy melon and hints of the tropics. On the palate, bright lifted fruit adds freshness to crème brûlée and soft toasty notes. The palate's full, lush mouthfeel produces a finish with great complexity and high acidity reminiscent of the great Graves Châteaux in Bordeaux.

WINEMAKER'S INSIGHT
As one of the most intriguing and serious white wines created in Napa Valley, our blanc is made in the style of a white Graves with fruit from our small, hillside sauvignon blanc vineyard. It is a complex offering, full of varietal purity with plenty of power and concentration. During a recent tasting, winemaker Philippe Melka exclaimed, "I can't wait to taste this wine in ten years!"

TECHNICAL DATA

APPELLATION: St. Helena
COMPOSITION: 100% sauvignon blanc
MATURATION: Aged for 20 months in Saury immersion barrels
CELLARING: Enjoy now and over the next seven to 12 years
WEBSITE: www.vineyard29.com

LEARN MORE

Learn more about Vineyard 29.

ZD Wines — RUTHERFORD

ZD Wines was founded by two aerospace engineers involved in the 1960s space race, Gino Zepponi and Norman deLeuze. The "ZD" of ZD Wines has two meanings: the obvious, the initials of the partners, and the inspirational: "Zero Defects," a quality control program used to build rocket engines. Since 1969, three generations of the deLeuze family have worked diligently to produce world-class Napa Valley wines. Based in Rutherford, ZD Wines is recognized as one of Napa's finest producers of chardonnay, pinot noir, and cabernet sauvignon. The winery also produces Rosa Lee's Whim, a wine that consumers look forward to each year because the varietal changes.

ABOVE: ZD's iconic rock sign, which has become a landmark for those traveling Napa Valley's Silverado Trail, is an enduring symbol of world-class wine.

FACING PAGE: A stone fountain adorns the entrance to ZD's tasting room.
Photographs by M. J. Wickham

ZD RESERVE CHARDONNAY

GOURMET PAIRINGS
A customer favorite, Mustards Grill crab cakes pair perfectly with the rich and wonderfully balanced chardonnay.

TASTING NOTES
Aromas of pear, orange blossom, lime zest, and sweet vanilla mingle with a palate bursting with bright fruit, lively acidity, and subtle toasty oak.

WINEMAKER'S INSIGHT
The chardonnay grapes are hand-harvested from ZD's organically certified Carneros Estate vineyard at optimal maturity and 100-percent barrel fermented in our cellar, kept at a chilly 48 degrees during fermentation. The long, cool fermentation preserves the vibrant tropical and clean citrus aromas while slowing the process enough to add a toasty, creamy intensity. The final wine is full of flavor with a balance of forward fruit and bright natural acidity.

TECHNICAL DATA

APPELLATION: Carneros
COMPOSITION: 100% chardonnay
MATURATION: 100% barrel fermented, 10% new oak; aged for 15 months in barrel
CELLARING: Three to five years
WEBSITE: www.zdwines.com

WATCH A VIDEO

CEO and winemaster Robert deLeuze introduces what the winery seeks from every bottle of its Reserve Chardonnay, from the Carneros vineyard to the winemaking techniques.

ZD Wines has two organically farmed vineyards. The Rutherford vineyard, planted to cabernet sauvignon, sits adjacent to the winery. The Carneros Estate, planted to pinot noir and chardonnay, has a refurbished 1890s house and eco-friendly barn on the property.

Norman's wife and co-founder, Rosa Lee, and family operate the winery. The second generation is represented by CEO and winemaster Robert, administrative director Julie, and president Brett; third-generation siblings are assistant winemaker Brandon and Jill, in sales. The deLeuze family works closely with winemaker Chris Pisani to produce wines that exceed the founders' vision. ZD Wines, having graced White House dinner menus and garnered hundreds of awards over the years, has become synonymous with quality, consistency, and style.

ABOVE LEFT: Wildflowers color the entrance to ZD's Carneros Estate Vineyard beside a state-of-the-art, environmentally conscious, solar-powered barn.

TOP: The family—Robert, Julie, Brandon, Rosa Lee, Jill, and Brett deLeuze—has been operating the winery for more than 40 years.

ABOVE: Visitors are welcome to walk into the ZD tasting room and experience true Napa Valley hospitality, or call ahead to set up a tour. *Photographs by M. J. Wickham*

FACING PAGE: *Photographs by M. J. Wickham*

Seguin Moreau Napa Cooperage, page 231

Taylor Lombardo Architects, page 235

Taylor Lombardo Architects, page 235

Seguin Moreau Napa Cooperage

NAPA

The right barrel really does make the wine; the wood functions as an essential enological tool. Oak softens and subdues wine's natural aggressive tannins, so the barrel preserves all the best elements of the wine while harmonizing the elements for greater complexity. At Seguin Moreau Napa Cooperage, the elite team is dedicated to the highest quality oak barrels crafted by master artisans who blend Old World traditions with the finest modern technologies. Tracing its history to Cognac—in 1972 Rémy Martin brought together the 1870-founded Seguin and 1838-founded Moreau cooperages—the company today has a presence in the world's major winemaking regions, including France, Australia, and Napa.

President François Peltereau-Villeneuve, a native of Reims, France, leads Seguin Moreau Napa Cooperage. An experienced production team of world-class coopers, classically trained in France and Scotland, produce Bordeaux-style, Burgundy-style, and 500-liter barrels. Each barrel, tank, and foudre is hand-toasted and hand-finished.

ABOVE: Seguin Moreau Napa Cooperage has stood at the entrance to the Napa Valley since its 1994 opening ceremony.

FACING PAGE: The flame toasts and caramelizes the sugars of the American oak U-STAVE™ barrel.
Photographs by M. J. Wickham

Seguin Moreau considers it of paramount importance to not only preserve and follow ancestral knowledge about barrel-making, but also to conduct scientific research and ascertain types of barrels ideally suited for a particular varietal. Sustainable practices receive a focus as well; some of the cooperage's barrel range is available CarbonNeutral®, with CO_2 emissions reduced to net zero throughout barrel production. Seguin Moreau Napa Cooperage is truly on the cutting edge of wine barrels.

ABOVE: One barrel has been shaped and is ready for bousinage, while another toasts for aromatics.

RIGHT: The ICÔNE barrel series is iconic. Elegance barrel oak is selected for certain chemical compounds and coopered for utmost consistency and quality. A plaque affixed nearly 20 years ago celebrates the cooperage's proud history in both France and Napa Valley.

FACING PAGE TOP: After the mise en rose, or raising, the barrels await an initial fire for shaping and bending.

FACING PAGE BOTTOM: President François Peltereau-Villeneuve heads the cooperage. On any given day, he will converse with employees in French, English, and Spanish.
Photographs by M. J. Wickham

WATCH A VIDEO

President François Peltereau-Villeneuve discusses the advantages of Seguin Moreau Napa Cooperage's ICÔNE barrel line.

Taylor Lombardo Architects

SAN FRANCISCO

Taylor Lombardo Architects is an award-winning architecture and land planning firm with offices in San Francisco and Napa Valley. In addition to a large number of projects in California, the firm has completed projects throughout the United States and in China for an international presence. The firm specializes in custom homes and wineries of all sizes and styles, tailored specifically to the needs of each site owner. Taylor Lombardo Architects has designed over 30 wineries, including Silver Oak Cellars, Nickel and Nickel Winery, and Kelly Fleming Wines. The firm also has extensive experience in hotel, retail, and restaurant design. Partners Tom Taylor and Maurice Lombardo are the primary contacts and remain very hands-on throughout every project. Taylor Lombardo Architects' philosophy maintains that the firm works closely with the owner, ensuring that each project is a creation specific to the individual desires and requirements of the project at hand.

The firm's design approach is one of creating site-sensitive and environmentally responsible structures that are at once timeless, innovative, and enduring.

ABOVE: The outdoor tasting area at Kelly Fleming Wines.
FACING PAGE: The exterior of Kelly Fleming Wines.
Photographs by Adrian Gregorutti

Careful attention to architectural scale, proportion, detailing, and material selection ensures the design will be true to the style desired. Integrating sustainable materials with state-of-the-art technology allows the firm to create both traditional and modern designs that meet all the challenges of today's green, energy-efficient requirements, without compromises to style, comfort, or beauty.

TOP: Silver Oak Cellars' hospitality building.
Photograph by Adrian Gregorutti

ABOVE: The historic Gleason Barn at Nickel and Nickel Winery.
Photograph by Adrian Gregorutti

RIGHT: Nickel and Nickel Winery's south fermentation building.
Photograph by Adrian Gregorutti

FACING PAGE TOP: The conference room at Silver Oak Cellars.
Photograph by Adrian Gregorutti

FACING PAGE BOTTOM LEFT: A view of the Glass Wine Room at Silver Oak Cellars.
Photograph by Jason Liske

FACING PAGE BOTTOM RIGHT: Interior view of the wine cave at Kelly Fleming Wines.
Photograph by Adrian Gregorutti

NAPA VALLEY TEAM
ASSOCIATE PUBLISHER: Carla Bowers
ASSOCIATE PUBLISHER: Peter Bowers
ART DIRECTOR: Emily A. Kattan
EDITOR: Megan Winkler
EDITOR: Sarah Tangney
MANAGING PRODUCTION COORDINATOR: Kristy Randall
TRAFFIC SUPERVISOR: Drea Williams

HEADQUARTERS TEAM
PUBLISHER: Brian G. Carabet
PUBLISHER: John A. Shand
GRAPHIC DESIGNER: Jen Ray
GRAPHIC DESIGNER: Lauren Schneider
MANAGING EDITOR: Lindsey Wilson
EDITOR: Nicole Pearce
DEVELOPMENT & DISTRIBUTION SPECIALIST: Rosalie Z. Wilson
ADMINISTRATIVE COORDINATOR: Amanda Mathers
ADMINISTRATIVE ASSISTANT: Aubrey Grunewald

PANACHE PARTNERS, LLC
CORPORATE HEADQUARTERS
1424 Gables Court
Plano, TX 75075
469.246.6060
www.panache.com

Chappellet Vineyard & Winery, page 51

INDEX

Beaulieu Vineyard 13
1960 St. Helena Highway
Rutherford, CA 94573
707.967.5233
www.bvwines.com

Blankiet Estate 17
PO Box 2100
Yountville, CA 94599
707.963.2001
www.blankiet.com

Cakebread Cellars 25
8300 St. Helena Highway
Rutherford, CA 94573
800.588.0298
www.cakebread.com

Castello di Amorosa 33
4045 North St. Helena Highway
Calistoga, CA 94515
707.967.6272
www.castellodiamorosa.com

Caymus Vineyards 43
8700 Conn Creek Road
Rutherford, CA 94573
707.967.3010
www.caymus.com

Chappellet Vineyard & Winery 51
Pritchard Hill
St. Helena, CA
707.963.7136
www.chappellet.com

David Arthur Vineyards 57
210 Long Ranch Road
St. Helena, CA 94574
707.963.5190
www.davidarthur.com

Del Dotto Winery 61
1445 St. Helena Highway South
St. Helena, CA 94574
707.963.2134
www.deldottovineyards.com

Domaine Carneros 69
1240 Duhig Road
Napa, CA 94581
707.257.0101
www.domainecarneros.com

Fantesca Estate & Winery 73
2920 Spring Mountain Road
St. Helena, CA 94574
707.968.9229
www.fantesca.com

Frog's Leap 79
PO Box 189
Rutherford, CA 94573
707.963.4704
www.frogsleap.com

Gargiulo Vineyards 83
575 Oakville Cross Road
Napa, CA 94558
707.944.2770
www.gargiulovineyards.com

Grgich Hills Estate 89
1829 St. Helena Highway
Rutherford, CA 94573
800.532.3057
www.grgich.com

Heitz Wine Cellars 95
500 Taplin Road
St. Helena, CA 94574
707.963.3542
www.heitzcellar.com

Hill Family Estate 103
6512 Washington Street
Yountville, CA 94599
707.944.9580
www.hillfamilyestate.com

Inglenook 109
1991 St. Helena Highway
Rutherford, CA 94573
707.968.1100
www.inglenook.com

Joseph Phelps Vineyards 113
200 Taplin Road
St. Helena, CA 94574
800.707.5789
www.josephphelps.com

Keenan Winery 117
3660 Spring Mountain Road
St. Helena, CA 94574
707.963.9177
www.keenanwinery.com

Kenzo Estate 123
3200 Monticello Road
Napa, CA 94558
707.254.7572
www.kenzoestate.com

Morlet Family Vineyards & Winery . . .129
2825 St. Helena Highway North
St. Helena, CA 94574
707.967.8690
www.morletwines.com

Mumm Napa 135
8445 Silverado Trail
Rutherford, CA 94573
800.686.6272
www.mummnapa.com

O'Connell Family Vineyard 141
4104 Dry Creek Road
Napa, CA 94558
415.425.3639
www.gabriellewine.com

Peju Province Winery 147
8466 St. Helena Highway
Rutherford, CA 94573
707.963.3600
www.peju.com

Robert Mondavi Winery 153
7801 St. Helena Highway
Oakville, CA 94562
707.967.6124
www.robertmondaviwinery.com

Rombauer Vineyards 159
3522 Silverado Trail
St. Helena, CA 94574
707.963.5170
www.rombauer.com

Round Pond Estate 165
875 Rutherford Road
Rutherford, CA 94573
888.302.2575
www.roundpond.com

Seguin Moreau Napa Cooperage 231
151 Camino Dorado
Napa, CA 94558
707.252.3408
www.seguinmoreaunapa.com

Shafer Vineyards 169
6154 Silverado Trail
Napa, CA 94558
707.944.2877
www.shafervineyards.com

Sherwin Family Vineyards 173
4060 Spring Mountain Road
St. Helena, CA 94574
707.963.1154
www.sherwinfamilyvineyards.com

Signorello Estate 177
4500 Silverado Trail
Napa, CA 94558
707.255.5990
www.signorelloestate.com

Silver Oak Cellars 181
915 Oakville Cross Road
Oakville, CA 94562
707.944.8808
www.silveroak.com

Silverado Vineyards 187
6121 Silverado Trail
Napa, CA 94558
707.257.1770
www.silveradovineyards.com

Spring Mountain Vineyard 193
2805 Spring Mountain Road
St. Helena, CA 94574
707.967.4188
www.springmountainvineyard.com

Staglin Family Vineyard 199
PO Box 680
Rutherford, CA 94573
707.963.3994
www.staglinfamily.com

Taylor Lombardo Architects 235
529 Commercial Street, Suite 400
San Francisco, CA 94111
415.433.7777
www.taylorlombardo.com

Trefethen Family Vineyards 205
1160 Oak Knoll Avenue
Napa, CA 94558
866.895.7696
www.trefethen.com

Twomey Cellars 211
1183 Dunaweal Lane
Calistoga, CA 94515
800.505.4850
www.twomey.com

Vineyard 7&8 215
4028 Spring Mountain Road
St. Helena, CA 94574
707.963.9425
www.vineyard7and8.com

Vineyard 29 219
2929 Highway 29 North
St. Helena, CA 94574
707.963.9292
www.vineyard29.com

ZD Wines .225
8383 Silverado Trail
Napa, CA 94558
707.963.5188
www.zdwines.com

Heitz Wine Cellars, page 95